INCREDIBLE ASCENTS TO EVEREST

Over the years, Everest has claimed many lives. Despite this, hundreds of climbers throng to the mountain every year in the hope of making it to the very top. Seen here are unidentified mountaineers descending from the summit of Everest in 2009.

Page 1: Tenzing Norgay on the summit of Mount Everest on 29 May 1953 waving the flags of the United Nations, Nepal, India and Great Britain, after becoming the first person, along with Edmund Hillary to scale Mount Everest.

CELEBRATING 60 YEARS OF THE FIRST SUCCESSFUL ASCENT

INCREDIBLE ASCENTS TO EVEREST

Sumati Nagrath

Foreword by Tom Whittaker

Interlink Books

An imprint of Interlink Publishing Group, Inc.
Northampton, Massachusetts

First published in 2013 by

INTERLINK BOOKS
An imprint of Interlink Publishing Group, Inc.
46 Crosby Street, Northampton, Massachusetts 01060
www.interlinkbooks.com

Library of Congress Cataloging-in-Publication Data available

ISBN 978-1-56656-941-5

Editors: Priya Kapoor and Renu Rao
Book design: Bonita Vaz-Shimray
Production: Shaji Sahadevan
Printed and bound in Singapore

10 9 8 7 6 5 4 3 2 1

*The Nepalese Himalayan region surrounding Mt Everest is
breathtaking. Seen here is the fluted peak above Nare Glacier seen
from Mingbo La in the Sagarmatha National Park.*
Following pages: *In his effort to forge the strongest and most able
team, Col John Hunt drew climbers from the entire Commonwealth
and included Sherpa men as equal climbing partners. Seen here is the
entire 1953 expedition team.*

CONTENTS

Foreword
TOM WHITTAKER

Almost lost in the vastness of the Ballroom in Buckingham Palace, I heard my name being announced, "Mr Thomas Whittaker" and moved forward across an acre of red carpet as the announcer continued, "For service to mountaineering and to people with disabilities." I bowed and approached the dais on which the diminutive form of Her Majesty Queen Elizabeth II stood.

Leaning forward she deftly pinned my "Badge" (as Georgia my seven-year-old daughter referred to my award) to my jacket lapel and surveyed her handiwork with satisfaction.

"Now, Mr Whittaker, I understand you are the very first person with a disability to climb Mount Everest."

"Yes, Your Majesty, but it took three tries over eight years to get to the top!"

"You must have been jolly proud...?"

"The thing I was proudest of was that I climbed it on exactly the same terms any serious mountaineer would, Ma'am. I was not on a commercial expedition or dragged up the mountain by able bodied guides. I was the expedition leader and my teammates and I climbed it on our own merits."

After a moment's reflection the 80-year-old monarch's reply cut to the heart of mountaineering.

"Yes," she said, "Style is so important, isn't it?"

Battered by the elements, in rarefied air, mountaineers seek their summits in the world's most hostile environs. In wind and snow, on rock and ice, they strive upwards. Their labours have no essential purpose; they're of no earthly value. There is no one to watch, no adoring public, no accolades. Financially, it's often ruinous. Why, then, do we do it?

The driving force behind mountaineering is humankind's need to sustain the soul through adventure.

This page: *Whittaker's MBE medal.*
Facing page: *Tom Whittaker seen here with his daughters Lizzie and Georgia after receiving the Most Magnificent Order of the Member of the British Empire (MBE) from Queen Elizabeth II in 2006.*

Facing page and right: *Made of metal and hard plastic, Whittaker's prosthesis is custom designed to give him the ability to flex the rubber-bottomed metal plate that acts as the foot, much like a kitchen spatula.*

Following pages: *Animals too have a tough time on the slopes of Everest. Seen here, yaks avoiding a crevasse on their way down East Rongbuk Glacier on Mount Everest.*

In mountaineering, the summit is typically the objective and one's measure of success. However, as George Mallory and Sandy Irvine's poignant story attests, the summit is not the finish line. That's always back in the safety of Base Camp.

Paradoxically, it is not the summit that defines the achievement but the journey to (or in Yuichiro Miura's case from) the summit. The audacity of the undertaking and the manner in which it is executed determines its significance and how your peers will judge the achievement.

However, it is the act of upholding the "style" of mountaineering that creates the quality of adventure that is soul sustaining. Personal gains take place when the integrity and harshness of the outer journey drives us within. It is only when we are impelled to reach beyond the perceived limits of our being, without compromising our standards, that the conditions for growth prevail. The rewards are in self-awareness and confidence that comes from being tested, and enduring.

The stories in these pages are of this calibre and all take place on an insatiable mountain that gobbles up money, resources and lives.

If you're like me and love to learn but hate being taught then "have I got some coal for your furnace" ... because as Sir Arthur Conan Doyle said, "Once you eliminate the impossible, whatever remains, no matter how improbable, must be the truth."

The inspiration and truth in the pages of this book is the stuff to light a prairie fire in your veins. And, once lit, who knows what summits you will reach!

Keep climbing to your dreams.

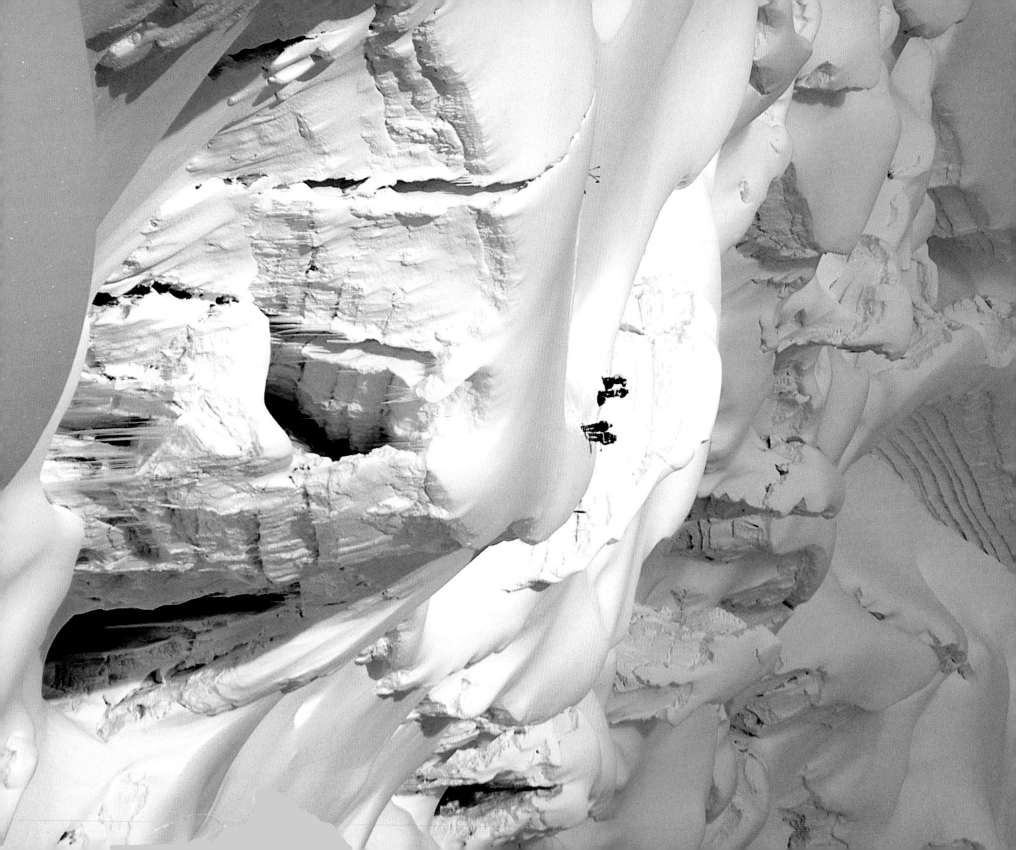

Introduction
MOUNT EVEREST: THE MOUNTAIN MADNESS

Mount Everest is an experiment of nature.

Standing 29,029 feet (8848 m) above sea level, the mountain is just about the maximum height to which human beings can climb. Any higher, and the atmospheric conditions would make it impossible for anyone to breathe and survive, let alone scale the peak of the world's tallest mountain. Life simply would not sustain. Already, the upper reaches of the mountain, or the expanse above the altitude of 26,246 feet (8000 m) is called the "Death Zone". The extremely low density of air at this elevation implies a severely reduced oxygen level which leads to immediate and rapid physiological deterioration. Severe altitude sickness sets in; debilitating the mind and body to such an extent that death becomes a very real possibility.

Yet, over the course of the last 90 years, thousands of men, women and even teenagers have thronged to Mount Everest, hoping to make it to the very top of this still growing mountain. What is it about climbing Mount Everest that makes people brave the really thin air, the treacherously deceptive terrain, and the very real and ever present danger of death?

"Everest for me, and I believe for the world, is the physical and symbolic manifestation of overcoming odds to achieve a dream," says Tom Whittaker, the first disabled person to summit Mount Everest.

In a May 2011 interview to Chinese TV channel New Tang Dynasty Television, Elizabeth Hawley, who since the 1960s has documented every single ascent that has taken place in the Nepalese Himalayas, shares the thought. She says that while "bragging rights" could be a reason why people set out on this quest, "the main reason is some people just like climbing, they just like the challenge to themselves, pushing themselves as far as they can go, seeing how far they can go."

Today, Mount Everest attracts the attention of millions of people across the world. Anything

Nepalese families have, over the years, accounted for the bulk of the Sherpa men for the Everest expeditions; their original semi-nomadic lifestyle has changed because of the money this has brought in.

Facing page (left): *Theodolite is perhaps the most famous of the tools used in the Great Trigonometric Survey of India; it also weighed over half a ton and needed a dozen men to carry it.*

Facing page (right): *Former Surveyor General of India George Everest, in whose honour the peak is named, was himself against this naming, because, as per norm, all mountains have been called by their traditional names.*

that happens on its slopes is news—from the people who climb it, to the people who fail to make it, to the environmental threat to its fragile ecology, to the piles of rubbish at base camp, to the bodies that litter its icy slopes, to the increased commercialisation of expeditions, to the increasing spectacles on the summit. It's noisy there now. There are "traffic jams" and "gridlocks" during climbing season. Many professional mountaineers refuse to return to Everest, eschewing it in favour of other, lesser known peaks.

Yet, for nearly sixty million years the mountain stood in stony silence; interrupted occasionally only by the gushing sounds of gale force winds, the muffled thumps of falling rocks

on thick blankets of snow and the thundering of unpredictable avalanches.

For centuries, the rarely visible pristine white peak of this geographical giant was home to the gods. It represented the unknown; the power of nature. With language, came the naming. No one knows when it was first called so, but the mountain was now Chomolungma—"Goddess Mother of the World". Human trespass was prohibited. Gods could not be disturbed; they would be angry, their wrath without mercy.

Meanwhile, in other parts of the world, the insatiable thirst for adventure had led humans to sail the high seas, conquer other countries, claim the sky and reach the poles. This latest of geographical novelties came to the attention

of Western explorers as late as 1841 when Sir George Everest, Surveyor General of India, first recorded the location of what was then termed as Peak b. A decade later Peak b was measured, renamed Peak XV and declared to be the world's highest mountain, its height determined as 29,002 feet (8840 m). Christened Mount Everest, in honour of Sir George in 1865, the mountain's height was later adjusted to 29,029 feet or 8848 metres.

The mountain captured the imagination of adventurers and explorers across the world, with each wanting to get to the top of Mount Everest first. In particular, it became an obsession of the British, who were reeling from the after-effects of the First World War and fast losing

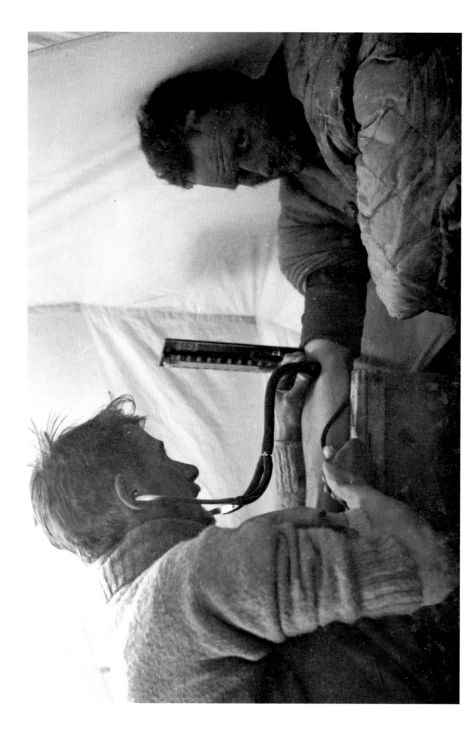

their imperial grandeur. Narrowly beaten by American and Norwegian explorers to the North and South Pole respectively, Mount Everest now represented the "third pole" for the British. Conquering it would bring with it a validation of their valour.

With the earliest expeditions in 1921, 1922 and 1924, it was the British who set in motion the explorations that would finally lead to the first successful summit of Mount Everest by Sir Edmund Hillary and Tenzing Norgay in 1953.

This book captures the extraordinary stories of ordinary men and women who have risked their physical, emotional and financial well-being to make the momentous and perilous climb to the top of the world's tallest mountain. In the process, each one of them has redefined the limits of what was thought possible till then. They have challenged stereotypes, defied conventions and beaten all odds to stand atop the summit of Mount Everest, and then make it back down safely.

Since Nepal was closed to foreigners in the first half of the twentieth century, the first expeditions made their way up the northern face of the mountain via Tibet. For the earliest explorers, setting foot on the mountain was no different from landing on the moon. There was very little that was known about the effects of extremely high altitudes on human physiology; it was an entirely unknown terrain—no one knew what to expect. In addition, the clothing and the equipment was both flimsy and cumbersome. Despite this, indomitable men such as George Mallory and Andrew Irvine set out—from never before reached altitudes—in pursuit of the elusive summit. Mallory and Irvine disappeared on the afternoon of 8 June 1924, and till today it is not known if they actually made it to the top of Mount Everest.

Politics once again changed the nature of Everest expeditions. Following the invasion by China, Tibet closed its borders to all foreigners in 1949, while at the same time Nepal began to allow them in. It meant that those in the quest for Everest now had to forge a new route, via the South side.

J.B. Noel maintained meticulous visual records of the 1922 and 1924 expeditions, which provide a rich archival history of what these early efforts entailed. He is seen here kinematographing the 1922 ascent from Chang La.

Facing page: *The careful monitoring of the climbers' blood pressure and other vitals was part of the expedition routine from the very beginning. Seen here, Charles Warren taking Eric Shipton's blood pressure during the 1938 expedition.*

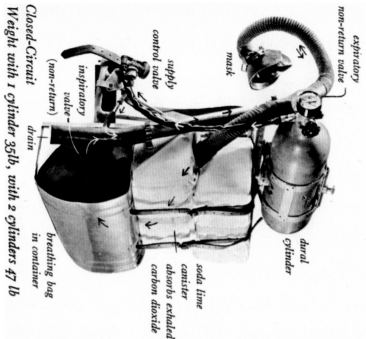

Closed-Circuit
Weight with 1 cylinder 35lb, with 2 cylinders 47 lb

expiratory non-return valve — mask — supply control valve — inspiratory valve (non-return) — dural cylinder — drain — soda lime canister absorbs exhaled carbon dioxide — breathing bag in container

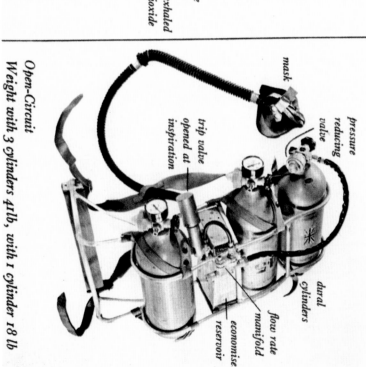

Open-Circuit
Weight with 3 cylinders 41lb, with 1 cylinder 18 lb

pressure reducing valve — mask — trip valve opened at inspiration — dural cylinders — flow rate manifold — economiser reservoir

A controversial choice at the time, Col John Hunt proved to be an extremely able leader of the 1953 expedition team. His detailed record keeping is visible here in his comparisons of the open and closed circuit oxygen equipment in his 1954 book Our Everest Adventure: The Pictorial History from Kathmandu to the Summit.

Facing page: *While Mount Everest is the most famous peak in the Nepalese Himalayas, the region is full of challenging climbs. Seen here are mountaineers climbing up the Imja Tse, also known as the Island Peak.*

Following in the footsteps of the courageous pioneers, who had carefully reconnoitred and mapped the hitherto unknown terrain of the mountain, were better equipped and better informed mountaineers. Part of the 1953 British Everest Expedition, Edmund Hillary and Tenzing Norgay created history on 29 May 1953 by becoming the first men to stand on top of the world's highest mountain, opening a floodgate of climbers who have thronged the slopes of Everest in the 60 years following their feat.

While Mallory, Irvine, Hillary and Tenzing Norgay are the giants of Everest history, no less important are the Sherpa people on whose backs, literally, the mountain has been scaled time and again. The remarkable "people of the East" are renowned and recognised for their prowess in the mountains and their unique physiological constitution that allows them to remain resilient at high altitudes.

With the mantle of the "first" belonging to Hillary and Tenzing Norgay, those attempting to create Everest history now had to do something different, something unique. One such person was the Japanese extreme skier, Yuichiro Miura, who, in 1970, became the first person to ski down

the slopes of Mount Everest. He then returned in 2003 to climb all the way to the summit, something that had eluded him the first time around. Five years later, he climbed to the very top once again, hoping to beat the record for the oldest person to climb Mount Everest. However, just a day before Miura reached the summit, Nepalese Min Bahadur Sherchan became the oldest person to summit the world's tallest mountain.

The record for the oldest woman to climb Mount Everest, nevertheless, belongs to a Japanese national, Tamae Watanabe, who first summited in 2002 at the age of 63. Ten years later, in 2012, she bettered her own record by

once again summiting the mountain. Watanabe's feat is, in part, due to the legacy of another Japanese female mountaineer, Junko Tabei. On 16 May 1975, Tabei defied all traditional gender stereotypes to become the first woman ever to stand on top of Mount Everest.

Also included in the book is Italian climber Reinhold Messner, considered by many to be the greatest mountaineer of all times. He is credited with redefining the parameters of mountaineering after climbing Mount Everest (along with Peter Habeler) without any supplemental oxygen in 1978 and then following that up two years later by making the first solo ascent to the peak. Messner took away all the paraphernalia that was part of the "siege" method of military style large expedition, and stripped climbing to its bare elements. He is the strongest advocate of the "alpine style", wherein the mountaineers climb alone, without supplemental oxygen and with everything they need on their backs.

Then there are individuals like Tom Whittaker, Mark Inglis and Mark Weihenmayer, who have not let their physical disabilities stand in the way of what they believe is possible. Tom Whittaker took the world by complete surprise when in 1998 he became the first disabled

The Khumbu Icefall is perhaps the most treacherous part of the Everest ascent from the south side; the ever-shifting river of ice changes with every season, catching many climbers by surprise. Seen here, team members of 1953 expedition reconnoitring in the Icefall.

Facing page: Documenting their climbs is an essential for all mountaineers, and it was more so for those attempting to get there first. Seen here is George Lowe changing a reel on his camera while resting in the Southeast Ridge at 27,300 feet (8321 m) in 1953.

Even when mountaineers climb in teams, they ultimately have to rely on their own inner reserves of physical, emotional and mental strength to make it right to the summit and return home safely.

Facing page: *The bright red and yellow tents make for a cheery contrast against the pristine white backdrop provided by the deep snow on the slopes of Mount Everest.*

person to reach the summit of Mount Everest. Eight years later, Inglis became the first double amputee to reach the very top. Weihenmayer created history in 2001 by becoming the first blind person to summit Everest. Their stories are of endurance, perseverance and, above all, courage. Criticised by some people for attempting to do something "irresponsible" that would put their and the lives of others in jeopardy, these individuals have proved their naysayers wrong. They have done so through a deep sense of commitment to themselves, their cause, and to the teammates who have helped them reach the top of the world.

Today, the climbing scene on Everest is very different. Hawley, in her book *A Statistical Analysis of Mountaineering in the Nepal Himalayas*, divides the climbing on Everest into three phases:

1. 1950-1969: the expeditionary period

2. 1970-1989: the transitional period

3. 1990-2009: the commercial period

The book lists 2009 as the end of phase 3, as that was the year it was published. However, the commercial period still continues and is posing a threat not just to the mountain but also to the climbers. While the ratio of deaths to successful climbs might have decreased over the years, the total number of deaths is going up, with the three most disastrous years being 1996, 2006 and 2012 with 15, 11 and 10 deaths respectively. There is

now a call for stricter regulations, which will allow only those with requisite experience to scale the mountain.

Looming five-and-a-half miles above the Earth's surface, the mountain evokes a certain madness. In the 90 years since the first expedition of 1921, over 3500 people have attempted the ascent of Mount Everest; close to 300 of them have died in the process. Yet more will come; driven by a thirst for adventure, a lust for fame, a desire to exorcise demons.

As Hillary famously said, "It's not the mountain we conquer but ourselves."

CHAPTER 1

Paving the Way
The Pre-1953 Everest Attempts

The First Seven Expeditions: 1921, 1922, 1924, 1933, 1935, 1936 and 1938, all British, all from the north side in Tibet

1939-50: Second World War and its aftermath stalls all Everest explorations

1949-50: Tibet closes its borders to foreigners, while Nepal opens its borders, making an expedition via the south side possible for the first time

1950: An Anglo-American reconnaissance mission led by Dr Charles Houston

1951: British expedition supported by the Alpine Club and the Royal Geographic Society

1952: Swiss Expedition sponsored by the Swiss Foundation for Alpine Research

" It stands to reason that men with any zest for mountaineering could not possibly allow Mount Everest to remain untouched. But climbing Mount Everest is no futile and useless performance of no satisfaction to anyone but the climbers. For the climbers are unwittingly carrying out an experiment of momentous consequence to mankind. They are testing the capacity of the human race to stand the highest altitudes on this earth which is its home. "

—**Sir Francis Younghusband** in the introduction to *Mount Everest the Reconnaissance*, by Charles Kenneth Howard-Bury, George H. Leigh-Mallory and A.F.R. Wollaston (1921)

The early expeditions were conducted in what came to be known as "siege" style and, apart from the climbers, included hundreds of porters carrying tons of equipment.

Members of the first British Everest Expedition became the first Western men to set foot on Everest in 1921. Seen here, Guy Henry Bullock showing the Sherpa men how to walk in snowshoes.

Facing page: *In 1922, the world's tallest mountain was still an enigma, despite the efforts of people like Captain J.B. Noel who made this Everest expedition film, the first-ever film on Everest in 1922.*

Tall, proud and pristine—the mountain had stood watch over the world for millions of years, witness to the great geographic and environmental shifts that shaped the Earth as we know it today. For centuries it stood there, unnoticed, undisturbed, unconquered.

Reverentially called Chomolungma by the Tibetans and Sagarmatha by the Nepalese, this mountain, this "roof of the world", was deemed to be a dwelling place of the gods by the local population. They believed that it was sacrilege to tread on this holy ground.

However, man's insatiable thirst for adventure was to soon change all that. It was in 1841, that Sir George Everest, Surveyor General of India, first recorded the location of what was termed as Peak b. The mountain was first surveyed in 1848 by a British expedition from a distance of around 110 miles and its elevation was calculated as 30,200 feet (9204.96 m). In 1852 came the Great Trigonometric Survey of India which determined that the hitherto obscure Himalayan peak, innocuously named Peak b, was most certainly the world's highest mountain. During 1854–56, Andrew Waugh, head of a British surveying team, made new observations with regard to Peak b and recalculated its elevation, this time with adjustments for barometric

pressure, temperature, and refraction. Renaming the mountain Peak XV, he set its elevation at an astonishingly accurate 29,002 feet (8840 m). Peak XV which was renamed in 1965 as Mount Everest, in honour of Sir George Everest by the Royal Geographical Society captured the world's imagination and very soon the idea of standing atop the world's highest mountain in the ultimate geographical feat gained huge currency among the leading explorers of the world—nations and individuals alike.

Nevertheless, 80 years would pass between Sir George's recording and the first official attempt to climb Mount Everest. The challenge in the early years was not so much about the height or the difficulty of terrain, but had more to do with access to the mountain. Mundane matters of permissions and regulations kept all climbing dreams at bay, with neither Tibet nor Nepal allowing foreigners into their respective countries.

It was only in 1920 that Tibet first opened its borders to outsiders and the British managed to secure permission for a reconnaissance party in 1921.

Prior to this, the interest in Mount Everest was kept alive by sporadic endeavours of a few intrepid individuals. The first photographs of Mount Everest showing any significant details were taken in 1904 by J. Claude

White. White was accompanying Sir Francis Younghusband to Tibet, who was under orders of the Viceroy of India, Lord Curzon, to try and mitigate possible Russian influence in the region through trade negotiations. This led Younghusband into Lhasa, enabling White to photograph the eastern side of Everest from Kampa Dzong, a distance of 94 miles (151 km). The first mapping of any possible route up the mountain is attributed to Natha Singh, a member of the British Indian Survey. He is said to have obtained permission to enter the Mount Everest region from the Nepalese side in 1907 and then mapped the Dudh Kosi valley right

up to the end of the Khumbu Glacier. In 1913, British explorer Captain John Noel is said to have "darkened his face, hair and skin" and then travelled undercover and illegally into Tibet as a native with the objective of making an initial survey of the region north of Mount Everest. He got to within 60 miles (nearly 100 km) of the peak before he had to turn back because he was confronted by a mountain range that he had failed to account for in his initial plans.

Meanwhile, with the North and South poles already conquered by the Americans and Norwegians respectively, the British were getting desperate to regain some of their fast fading imperial grandeur by becoming the first to conquer Mount Everest. In 1920, The Mount Everest Committee (MEC) was set up and a resolution passed, stating that an expedition would take place the following year with the objective of reconnaissance. A full-scale summit attempt was to be launched only the year after, that is, in 1922. In all, between 1921 and 1938, the MEC organised the first seven Mount Everest Expeditions, each one of them attempting to climb the mountain from the north side.

After much backdoor diplomacy, in 1921 a small private British expedition led by Colonel Charles Howard-Bury managed to secure

Quintessentially British, the gentlemen-climbers of the early expeditions would sit down at a makeshift dining table for breakfast every morning. Their food supplies are said to have included luxuries such as champagne and caviar.

Facing page: *Setting their eyes on Mount Everest for the first time was an overwhelming experience. Those who came in 1921 were determined to get to the very top, including George Leigh Mallory, who took this photograph.*

permission from the Dalai Lama to approach Mount Everest from the Tibetan side to map and explore the mountain's northern face. On 24 September 1921, after almost four months of exploration, two members of the First British Everest Reconnaissance Expedition, George Leigh Mallory and Guy Bullock, became the first climbers in the world to reach a height of approximately 23,000 feet (7000 m) on the North Col of Mount Everest via East Rongbuk. In the process they established the northern route up the mountain, supported by the mapping done by Oliver Wheeler. It has been recorded that from that height, Mallory was able to gauge a feasible route to the summit via the Northeast Ridge but felt that a more rested and fresh set of climbers would be able to achieve that feat.

As planned, the British were back a year later, this time determined to make a full assault to the summit. The Second British Everest Expedition to Mount Everest was led by General C.G. Bruce and it followed the same route as the 1921 expedition. Mallory was once again part of this team along with climbers George Finch, Geoffrey Bruce, Henry Morshead, Edward

Norton, and Howard Somervell. The first attempt for the summit was made on 22 May by Mallory, Norton, Somervell and Morshead. They managed to climb to 26,800 feet (8170 m) on the North Ridge before retreating. The following day Finch and Bruce made history by becoming the first climbers to reach a height of over 27,000 feet (8229 m). They were, however, using flimsy and cumbersome oxygen supplies and could not go higher. Later after a fresh snowfall, Mallory led a final assault on the summit on 7 June. However, this triggered an avalanche which claimed the lives of seven

Mount Everest inspired some inventive adventures, including the attempt by Marquis of Clydesdale to fly over the summit and take the first aerial photographs of the mountain.

Centre: *Clad in layers of cotton, wool and gabardine and shod in hobnailed leather boots, the pioneers braved the fiercest conditions without any of the present-day lightweight weather resistant clothing.*

Facing page: *Eleven years after the first expedition, climbing equipment and expedition formats remained unchanged. Ever particular about their appearance and general demeanour, the members of the 1933 British expedition are seen getting their hair cut and beards trimmed in an impromptu barbershop. The Sherpa porters often played multiple roles which included being cooks, valets and barbers.*

> ❝ We were deep inside the Himalayas when we first heard about the new reconnaissance of Everest. Someone had sent us a newspaper cutting, which came up with our mail-runner. It was exciting and disturbing news... What we'd do to get on a trip like that! We avidly read all the paper had to say. It explained how all the early expeditions to Everest had approached the mountain through Tibet and had tried to climb it up its northern slopes. There had been seven expeditions since the first one in 1921 but, though they'd performed unbelievable feats of courage and endurance, they hadn't got higher than a thousand feet from the top. It almost seemed as though there was some invisible barrier at 28,000 feet through which no man could go. And then, for a period of over 10 years, the mountain was left completely alone. ❞
>
> —**Sir Edmund Hillary talking about the expeditions to Everest which had preceded the one that he was part of in 1951**

Sherpas (the first recorded deaths on Mount Everest) leaving Mallory wracked with guilt.

In 1924, two years after his previous climb, Mallory returned as part of the third British expedition which was led by Major Edward Norton. Mallory and Bruce made the first summit bid on 1 June but had to abandon their attempt. On 4 June, climbing from the Northeast Ridge route, Norton became the first climber to

reach a height of 28,126 feet (8,570 m) without oxygen, a record that stood for the next 54 years. (It was broken by Reinhold Messner and Peter Habeler in 1978). After his climbing partner Somervell could no longer continue because of health reasons, Norton attempted a solo ascent to the summit across the Great Couloir on Everest's North Face. On 8 June, Mallory and Andrew "Sandy" Irvine set out on their summit bid, climbing without oxygen from their high camp at 26,700 feet (8,138 m). Their last reported sighting was by fellow climber Noel Odell, who saw them "going strong for the top" at 12.50 p.m. Mallory and Irvine never returned to camp; until today the climbing community wonders whether they were the first two men in the world to summit Mount Everest successfully. Even after the discovery of Mallory's body in 1999, the debate continues and the mystery endures.

Post Mallory and Irvine's disappearance, there was silence on the mountains for nearly a decade.

Facing page: *Climbing in large numbers and with heavy equipment often meant slow progress. Despite the fact that climbers had been on the mountain for a decade-and-a-half now, the mountain was still not fully known. Seen here, some members of the 1935 expedition take a break while ascending Mount Everest.*

Previous pages: *In the first half of the 20th century, Nepal was closed to foreigners. The early expeditions had no choice but to make their way through Tibet to the North face of Mount Everest. In 1924, Col Edward Norton led his team through the same route, but managed to get them higher than the previous two expeditions.*

Flights of Fancy

While any number of men were content with walking up to the top of the world, there were others who were a tad more adventurous and flamboyant. In 1933 Lucy, Lady Houston, a British millionaire and ex-showgirl, funded the Houston Everest Flight led by the Marquis of Clydesdale. The objective of the mission was to take the first ever aerial photographs of a completely unknown and unmapped terrain. Thus, the first flight over Mount Everest was by two British Westland biplanes powered by turbocharged Pegasus engines. While the planes, which took off from Purnea (present-day Bihar, India) managed to fly over the summit, they did not result in any usable photographs as the photographer blacked out due to a ruptured oxygen line.

Adventurists, in the early 1930s, like Maurice Wilson believed that they could crashland on the upper slopes of Mount Everest and then walk their way to the summit.

Pioneers such as George Mallory believed that using oxygen while climbing would somehow be "unsporting", but there were others like George Finch who were convinced that without oxygen the summit would always remain elusive. Seen here the 1924 team members practice using the oxygen equipment.

But with fears that American and German climbers might beat them to the top of Everest, the British were back once again after having successfully lobbied the Dalai Lama into giving permission.

In 1933, the Fourth British Expedition comprised a new generation of climbers such as Eric Shipton, Frank Smythe, P. Wyn Harris and Jack Longland under the leadership of Hugh Ruttledge. This expedition included a team of

Sherpas as well. The expedition set up camp on a ledge half-way up the Yellow Band at a height of 27,300 feet (8320 m). Despite some brave attempts without oxygen, none of the expedition members managed to get beyond Norton's high point. However, the expedition did find Andrew Irvine's ice axe at 27,690 feet (8440 m), east of the First Step.

Three more British expeditions followed: in 1935 (led by Eric Shipton and included Tenzing Norgay), 1936 (led by Hugh Ruttledge) and 1938 (led by H.W. Tillman), but each one was plagued by bad weather, preventing any serious bids for the ultimate summit prize.

The Second World War stalled any further

Spending months together in isolation from the rest of the world, often led to evenings of inventive entertainment, seen here Jack Longland pole jumping at Tengkye Dzong in 1933.

Facing page: *It was only in 1922 that the East Rongbuk Glacier was discovered by George Mallory. Seen here, a team member of the 1936 expedition attempts to cross a small crevasse using an ice axe.*

Previous pages: *Many of the ice caps that awed the early climbers no longer exist. Mountaineers like Apa Sherpa (who summitted Mount Everest for a record 21st time in May 2011, lament the effects of environmental deterioration on Mount Everest.*

attempts on Mount Everest as all elite climbing nations were caught up in the war and its aftermath. In 1947, Canadian-born Earl Denman attempted to illegally climb Everest from the North side along with Sherpas Ang Dawa and Tenzing Norgay. Despite near-arrests, inadequate equipment and poor health, the three managed to reach the foot of the North Col but turned back after realising that they could not go any further, hampered as they were by lack of resources and inferior equipment. The political landscape of the area began to change after China invaded Tibet in October 1950 and effectively ceased all outside contact with the world. Everest expeditions from the North were now prohibited. Meanwhile, the reverse was happening in Nepal, where after a palace revolution wherein the ruling Rana

family was overthrown, the government opened up to the West. Foreign expeditions were now allowed access to the southern side of Everest for the first time, perhaps paving the way for the first successful summit bid.

Two successive reconnaissance expeditions followed suit, the first in 1950, an Anglo-American venture, was led by Dr Charles Houston. They explored the base of the Khumbu Icefall and concluded that the route up into the Western Cwm was not a viable one. The second expedition was supported by the Alpine Club and the Royal Geographic Society and was led by Eric Shipton and included Edmund Hillary. After several delays, the 1951 expedition began its climb with the objective of scaling the Khumbu Icefall and entering the Western Cwm. However, once on the mountain, they assessed that the route

Facing page and above: *Many responsibilities of the Sherpa members of the expedition included laying fixed ropes and ladders and cooking meals. Appetite is one of the first casualties of high altitude climbing, with most climbers rarely being able to keep any food down.*

Previous pages: *The Sherpa porters and guides drawn from the villages of Tibet and Nepal remain an indispensable part of any climbing expedition even today.*

parts to the expedition, the Spring Attempt and the Post-Monsoon Attempt. The former was led by Dr E. Wyss-Dunant. The most successful of the climbers were Tenzing Norgay and Raymond Lambert, who made an attempt using oxygen but reached only an altitude of 28,210 feet (8595 m), managing to beat Norton's height record by only 84 feet (25 m). The second phase was led by G. Chevalley and once again included Lambert and Tenzing. This time, instead of climbing the Geneva Spur, the expedition pushed up the Lhotse Face and set up camp in South Col.

Though the onset of winter put a stop to all further climbing attempts, the groundwork for the 1953 summit conquest had already been laid.

up to the South Col was feasible and eventually pushed the route almost completely through to the top of the Icefall before retreating.

The most successful of the early expeditions arrived at the Everest Base Camp in 1952—the Swiss Expedition sponsored by the Swiss Foundation for Alpine Research. There were two

The 1953 British Expedition was led by Colonel John Hunt and comprised a number of experienced climbers including Edmund Hillary and the Sirdar of the Sherpas, Tenzing Norgay. The route through the Icefall was completed by 22 April and Camp VI was established at the foot of the Lhotse face at 23,000 feet (7000 m). The team was delayed for a number of reasons and finally reached the South Col via the Lhotse face, following in the footsteps of previous year's

The first question you will ask and which I must try to answer is this, 'What is the use of climbing Mount Everest?' and my answer must at once be, 'It is no use.' There is not the slightest prospect of any gain whatsoever. Oh, we may learn about the behaviour of the human body at high altitudes, and possibly medical men may from our observations do some accounting for the purposes of aviation. But otherwise nothing will come of it. We shall not bring back a single bit of gold or silver, not a gem, nor any coal or iron. We shall not find a single foot of earth that can be planted with crops to raise food. It is no use. So, if you cannot understand that there is something in man which responds to the challenge of this mountain and goes out to meet, that the struggle is the struggle of life itself upward and forever upward, then you won't see why we go. What we can get from this adventure is just sheer joy. And joy, is after all, the end of life. We do not live to eat and make money. We eat and make money to be able to enjoy life. That is what life means and what life is for.

—**George Leigh Mallory on what drove him to attempt the ascent of Mount Everest 1922**

Swiss expedition. On 29 May, over a month and one unsuccessful assault later, Hillary and Tenzing attempted a second assault. They left Camp IX which was set up at approximately 27,900 feet (8500 m) by 6.30 a.m. Five hours later, after negotiating the 40 foot (12 m) icy ascent (thereafter called the Hillary Step) they became the first known humans to reach the summit of Everest, earning themselves a place in world history.

These men climbed in tweed jackets and plain leather boots, armed with flimsy but cumbersome equipment and full of humour, grit and determination. There was little that was known about the debilitating physiological and psychological effects of extremely high altitudes on humans and yet these courageous individuals were willing to take a leap into the unknown, assured that what they would achieve at the end of this gruelling endeavour, would make it all worth it.

Though not vastly different from the equipment used in 1921, the successful expedition of 1953 did have better oxygen apparatus, which is believed to have helped Hillary and Tenzing reach the summit.
Left: *Mount Everest was Chomolungma, or Mother Goddess of the Earth, to Tibetans for centuries. Believing it to be the dwelling place of the gods, not one of them dared to climb to its summit till the arrival of Western explorers.*

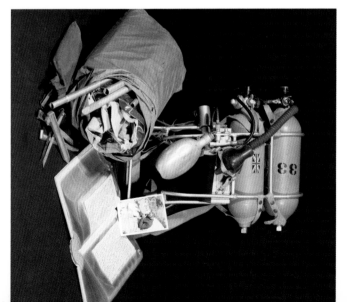

CHAPTER 2

1924

Mallory and Irvine
Were they the First?

George Leigh Mallory

Age at Time of Ascent: 38 years

Country of Origin: United Kingdom

Everest Feat: Could have been the first to reach the summit; body was found 75 years later at 8100 feet (2469 m)

The mystery endures

———

Andrew "Sandy" Irvine

Age at Time of Ascent: 22 years

Country of Origin: United Kingdom

Everest Feat: The first recorded "disappearance" on Everest. Body remains undiscovered till this day

“ There was a sudden clearing of the atmosphere and the entire summit ridge and the final peak of Everest were unveiled. My eyes became fixed on one tiny black spot silhouetted on a small snow crest beneath a rock step in the ridge; the black spot moved. Another black spot became apparent and moved up the snow to join the other on the crest. The first then approached the great rock step and shortly emerged at the top; the second did likewise. Then the whole fascinating vision vanished, enveloped in cloud once more. There was but one explanation. It was Mallory and his companion moving, as I could see even at that great distance, with considerable alacrity.... The place on the ridge referred to is the prominent rock step at a very short distance from the base of the final pyramid. ”

—**Noel Odell**, expedition member, 1924

The seriousness of what the earliest mountaineers on Everest were attempting was often peppered by moments of humour. Seen here, Howard Somervell (L), without trousers, Arthur Wakefield (C) with boots swung around his neck and a naked George Mallory (R), after fording a stream on the way up to the summit. Mallory could be described as a quirky Englishman with a streak of adventure and eccentricity, who also possessed a determination that few could boast of.

I t is one of the most enduring and tantalising mysteries of Everest lore: did George Leigh Mallory and Andrew "Sandy" Irvine reach the summit of Mount Everest before disappearing forever? This question continues to remain unanswered even 90 years after it was first raised. If the two of them did indeed reach the top of Mount Everest on 8 June 1924, as many mountaineers believe, it would mean that Mallory and Irvine would have beaten Edmund Hillary and Tenzing Norgay as the first people to summit the world's highest mountain by a good 29 years.

Mallory had ventured on the icy slopes of Everest twice before and was determined to climb it all the way to the top. His matter-of-fact approach to the mountain is evident from his, by now legendary, response to a reporter's question, "Because it's there".

A thorough British gentleman who hobnobbed with the avant garde Bloomsbury set, Mallory was also considered to be one of the finest mountaineers of his time—in fact one of the few handful British climbers to have survived the First World War.

Thus, when the team was being put together for the First British Everest Reconnaissance Expedition, Mallory's inclusion was an obvious one. Led by Colonel Charles Howard-Bury, the expedition arrived in Tibet in 1921 to attempt to scale the mountain from the northern side. After five months of reconnoitring at the base of the mountain, Mallory discovered the hidden East Rongbuk Glacier and its route to the base of the North Col. During this expedition, Mallory, along with Guy Bullock, became the first climber in the world to reach a height of approximately 23,000 feet (7000 m) before being forced back due to strong winds. The following year, Mallory was back again as part of the Second British Everest Expedition, this time under the leadership of General C.G. Bruce. The expedition followed the same route as the 1921 one. Mallory was joined by climbers George Finch, Geoffrey Bruce, Henry Morshead, Edward Norton, and Howard Somervell. On 22 May 1922 Mallory, Norton, Somervell and Morshead managed to climb up to a height of 26,800 feet (8170 m) on the North Ridge before having to retreat.

Mallory was a man on a mission. He was resolute about standing on top of the world's tallest mountain. Thus, after two unsuccessful attempts later he returned for the third—and what was to be his last—time to Mount Everest in 1924. Although initially led by General Bruce, the expedition was taken over by Colonel Edward Norton as the former contracted malaria. As a result, Mallory was promoted to climbing leader. Much of the team comprised members from the previous expedition, with two new additions, that of Noel Odell and the young graduate student from Oxford University, Andrew Irvine.

After months of acclimatisation, on 2 June, Mallory and Bruce set off for the first summit bid

Mallory's hobnailed leather boot was found intact with his body in May 1999 by the Mallory and Irvine Research Expedition led by Eric Simonson.
Facing page: *Mallory, climbing along with Edward Norton, reached a record height of 26,985 feet (8225 m) in 1922.*

Ensconced in layers of cotton and wool to protect themselves from the cold, these courageous pioneers wore nothing sturdier than thick gabardine jackets and hobnailed leather boots, at times giving the impression of being gentlemen out for a walk in the countryside rather than hardy climbers attempting to scale some of the world's most treacherous terrain.

On the morning of 8 June, kitted in similar gear, the 38-year-old Mallory, by now an Everest veteran, set out for a summit bid with the relatively novice and young Irvine from their high

from Camp IV on the North Col. However, the extreme cold and bitter winds combined with severe exhaustion, led them to abandon the effort and turn back. Two days later, climbing without oxygen, Norton and Somervell attempted their first summit bid. However, Somervell fell ill at about 28,000 feet (8534 m) and had to turn back. Norton carried on alone and reached a height of 28,126 feet (8,570 m), just 900 feet (275 m) short of the summit, before exhaustion forced him to turn back and join Somervell for the descent.

Mallory and Irvine were attempting to climb from the northern face. Seen here is the route they would have taken.

Facing page: *A very young Sandy Irvine was invited to join the 1953 expedition not just because of his remarkable athleticism, but also for his mechanical skills which enabled him to adapt and repair equipment with minimal resources.*

HIGHEST BIVOUAC
N.E. SHOULDER
27,000 FT.

WINDY RIDGE CAMP

MALLORY and IRVINE
LAST SEEN HERE
28,400 FT.

ODELL THROUGH HIS TELESCOPE SEES THE TWO MEN
WITHIN 600 FEET OF SUMMIT.

SUMMIT
29,000 FT.

“ We saw the great mountain standing up from its base at the end of [the valley], a more glorious sight than I can attempt to describe... the most steep ridges and appalling precipices that I have ever seen... I can't tell you how it possesses me, and what a prospect it is. ”

—George Leigh Mallory on seeing Everest for the first time in 1921

The Companion: Andrew "Sandy" Irvine

Sandy Irvine's name seems to be added on as an after-thought whenever there is talk of the Mallory and Irvine mystery. However, Irvine was an equal and deserving partner of Mallory.

Born on 8 April 1902, Irvine was one of six siblings—five boys and one girl. Good looking, athletic and a rower par excellence, Irvine made his way to Merton College at Oxford University. While at Merton College, he helped Oxford University's rowing team beat the Cambridge University team not once, but twice. As part of Merton College, he also went on the Arctic Expedition to Spitsbergen, and it was his exploits there that brought him to the attention of Noel Odell, who had been invited to be part of the Third British Everest Expedition. In fact, Odell, who finally recommended that Irvine be included in the Everest Expedition, had also met him previously on top of the 3000 feet (914 m)-high Welsh mountain of

Foel Grach. Legend has it that Odell and his wife, who had both trekked up on foot, were shocked to find out that Irvine had ridden his motorbike all the way up.

Besides being an all star-athlete, Irvine was also a mechanical genius. His engineering skills had already been tested during the First World War at the war office, where he was known to be able to improve the functionality of almost any equipment.

Commenting on the inclusion of this remarkable young man in the Everest expedition, General Bruce wrote in the *Times* on 17 March 1924, "The experiment of the expedition is Mr Irvine... His record at Spitsbergen last year and his really remarkable physique, to say nothing of his reputation as a general handyman, justify the experiment we are making in exposing one of his tender years to the rigours of Tibetan travel. We entertain no fears on this account..."

Facing page: *Mallory was perhaps the most accomplished British mountaineer of his generation. Seen here, bathing at Rongli. The 1921 expedition passed through Rongli in Sikkim, while on their way to Kathmandu.*

camp at 26,900 feet (8199 m). Questions have been asked about Mallory's choice of 22-year-old Irvine as a climbing partner over the other more experienced team-members. Some schools of thought believe it was because of Irvine's mechanical skills. Mallory, who had disavowed the use of oxygen in his first two climbs in the name of fair play and sportsmanship, was now beginning to think that it was perhaps impossible to scale Everest without supplemental oxygen. Since it was not known how the apparatus would behave at such extreme heights, Irvine, given his expertise with the equipment, was the obvious choice. However, another school of thought holds that it could simply be that they decided they wanted to go up together.

Climbing in the traditional way and carrying Irvine's modified oxygen apparatus for higher altitude, Mallory and Irvine were last sighted by fellow climber Noel Odell, who saw them "going strong for the top" at about 12.50 p.m. Mallory and Irvine never returned to camp and left in their wake the longest lasting Everest mystery—Were they the first men in the world to summit Mount Everest successfully?

Odell's account of the exact spot of their sighting wavered, compounding the mystery. Initially having identified them as standing on the Second Step, Odell later said that Mallory and Irvine were in fact seen standing on the First Step.

There are several theories about what could possibly have happened to them. One of the possible scenarios posits that after reaching the First Step and realising the treacherous nature of the traverse to the Second Step, Mallory decided to make a go of it alone. However, deciding that the conditions were not suitable, he turned back and along with Irvine decided to take photographs of the route from the First to the Second step. The theory further argues that it was on this descent from the First Step that they were hit by a severe snow squall, leading one

Even 90 years after he was last seen climbing towards the summit with Irvine, Mallory remains one of the most enigmatic figures of Everest history. His life was captured in a fictionalised account by Jeffrey Archer in Paths of Glory.

Facing page: In 1921 it was Mallory who first discovered the hidden East Rongbuk Glacier and its route to the base of the North Col.

Following pages: This is the famous last photograph of George Mallory and Sandy Irvine taken just before they left for the North Col in their summit bid.

Members of the first British Everest Expedition (1921) seen here, back row from L to R: Guy Bullock, Henry Morshead, Oliver Wheeler, George Leigh Mallory. Seated in front from L to R: A.M. Heron, A.R.F. Wollaston, Col Charles Howard-Bury and Harold Raeburn.

Facing page: *Mallory, who in Edmund Hillary's words had a "personal relationship with the mountain", was a mountaineer at heart. Seen here in 1909 on the Moine Ridge of the Aiguille Verte in France.*

Fourth British Everest Expedition, discovered an ice-axe believed to be Irvine's, at 27,920 feet (8,460 m), less than 1000 feet (304 m) short of the First Step. The discovery, however, failed to shed light on the actual movement of the duo and only served to fuel further speculations.

Several decades and a number of successful ascents later, the Eric Simonson-led Mallory & Irvine Research Expedition of 1999 discovered Mallory's remains at 26,750 feet (8150 m), on a line vertically below the ice axe position. The body was found to be remarkably well preserved with the remains of a rope still encircled around his waist, indicating that he and Irvine were tied together at the time that he fell. Mallory also had a puncture the size of a golf on his forehead, indicating a probable cause of death.

of them to slip, which explains the rope injuries found later on Mallory's body. There are others who maintain that it is possible that Mallory and Irvine separated after the fall due to the near white-out conditions of the squall.

It was not until nine years later that the first remains of Mallory and Irvine's climb were found. In 1933, Percy Wyn-Harris, part of the

Last Words

The last two notes written by Mallory on 7 June 1924, just a day before he disappeared, to his teammates are poignant, full of typical British cheer and understatement. They are perhaps the best tools to explain the pair's final movements.

His note to Odell reads:

Dear Odell,

We're awfully sorry to have left things in such a mess—our Unna cooker rolled down the slope at the last moment. Be sure of getting back to IV tomorrow in time to evacuate before dark as I hope to. In the tent I must have left a compass—for the Lord's sake rescue it, we are without. To here on 90 atmospheres for the two days so we'll probably go 2 cylinders, but it's a bloody load for climbing.

Perfect weather for the job,
Yours ever,
G Mallory

Mallory's body was found in 1999 and the artifacts on him were found remarkably preserved. These included old bills (facing page), tins of meat and lozenges (above). The world mourned the deaths of Mallory and Irvine and the dream and hopes they represented of a generation just coming out of the horrors of the First World War. What was, however, not found on Mallory was his wife Ruth's photograph, fuelling the belief that he had indeed reached the summit, where he had pledged to leave her photograph.

His second note was written to expedition photographer, John Noel:

Dear Noel,

We'll probably start early tomorrow (8th) in order to have clear weather.

It won't be too early to start looking out for us either crossing the rockband under the pyramid or going up skyline at 8 p.m.

Yours ever,

G Mallory

In his last letter to his wife, Ruth, Mallory wrote:

I'm quite doubtful if I shall be fit enough. But again I wonder if the monsoon will give us a chance. I don't want to get caught, but our three-day scheme from the Chang-La will give the monsoon a good chance. We shall be going up again the day after tomorrow. Six days to the top from this Camp.

Mallory and Irvine were last spotted by Noel Odell at 12.50 p.m. making their way up what he first described to be the Second Step. Odell later changed his account to the First Step. This is an artist's impression of that final sighting.

Facing page: *Months elapsed between arrival in Tibet and the ascent up Everest. Long periods were spent getting supplies in place and getting acclimatised to the altitude.*

Following pages: *While there had been some photographs of Everest before, those taken in 1921 provided the first real comprehensive views of the mountain and surrounding peaks.*

Finding Mallory's body seemed to have fanned the belief that he and Irvine did indeed summit the peak. Two crucial pieces of evidence are cited in favour of this argument. The first of these is that Mallory's daughter and other family members have steadfastly maintained that he carried a picture of his much beloved wife Ruth on his person with the intention of leaving it at the summit. No photo was found on his person and, given the excellent state of preservation of the body and the artefacts on it, the absence of the photo could possibly imply that he had managed to reach the summit and left the photograph there. The second piece of evidence that supports the theory is that Mallory's snow goggles were found in his pocket, suggesting that he died at night. It is plausible that he and Irvine had made a bid for the summit and were descending very late in the day because if they had turned back before reaching the summit, they would not have been out after nightfall.

There have also been possible sightings of Irvine's body. But the holy grail of Everest and mountaineering historians—the Vest Pocket Kodak camera that Irvine is supposed to have

WAS THE SUMMIT OF EVEREST REACHED?

Mr. Odell's Story, which is Now Being Told from the Lecture Platform

been carrying—still remains to be found. It is generally believed that if the camera is found and the film on it developed, it would once and for all bring the "did-they, did-they-not-summit" debate to a final conclusion.

On being asked to share his views on the mystery of Mallory and Irvine, Sir Edmund Hillary, is believed to have said: "I don't know whether Mallory and Irvine reached the summit... What I do know is that Tenzing Norgay and I were the first to get to the top and back down to the bottom again."

They may not have been the first to summit Everest, but Mallory and Irvine remain two of the most iconic figures of mountaineering history.

CHAPTER 3

1953

Edmund Hillary
and Tenzing Norgay
On Top of the World

Name: Edmund Percival Hillary

Age at Time of Ascent: 33

Country of Origin: New Zealand

Name: Tenzing Norgay

Age at Time of Ascent: 39

Country of Origin: Tibet/Nepal/India

Everest Feat: The first men in the world to stand on the summit of Mount Everest, bringing to conclusion over three decades of effort by the British.

❝ *Nobody climbs mountains for scientific reasons. Science is used to raise money for the expeditions, but you really climb for the hell of it.* **❞**

—**Sir Edmund Hillary**

....

The unlikely pair of 33-year-old Kiwi beekeeper Edmund Percival Hillary and 39-year-old Nepalese Sherpa Tenzing Norgay became the first men to set foot on the summit of Mount Everest on 29 May 1953.

Col John Hunt replaced the much loved and admired Eric Shipton as the expedition leader amidst much controversy. He however went on to build and manage the team in the most extraordinary fashion, earning the respect of all. Seen here with Tenzing Norgay, organising the payment of low altitude porters at Thyangboche.

Facing page: Having conquered Everest, Hillary and Tenzing were now heroes, their feat celebrated worldwide. They made it to the front cover of the Illustrated London News.

A t 11.30 a.m. on 29 May 1953, history was made when Edmund Hillary and Tenzing Norgay became the first people to stand on top of Mount Everest, the world's highest mountain. With their final step onto the summit, they brought to fruition decades worth of planning, toiling and dreaming, and made possible what until now was considered to lie in the realm of the impossible. Their success also ended a 30-year-old race amongst nations and individuals to reach the highest spot on Earth.

Hillary and Tenzing's magnificent achievement was marked by humour, an understated bold heroism and a genuine humility. Recounting his climb, Tenzing wrote: "My mountain did not seem to me a lifeless thing of rock and ice, but warm and friendly and living. She was a mother hen and the other mountains were chicks under her wings." Hillary's reaction was a little less spiritual. On their way down from the summit, they met their teammate and Hillary's long time friend, George Lowe, and Hillary is said to have famously exclaimed to him, "Well, George we've knocked the bastard off!"

The apparently odd pairing of the lanky New Zealander and the diminutive Sherpa was not accidental. They were both part of a well orchestrated effort by Colonel John Hunt,

the leader of the 1953 British Everest Expedition, to put together a team of world-class climbers to achieve the quest for Everest. Between 1921 and 1952, eight major expeditions had failed to reach the summit. Also, by 1953 Great Britain no longer had a monopoly over the mountain, with permissions being granted by the Nepalese authorities to expeditions from other countries. In fact, the Swiss Expedition of 1952 had come much too close to the summit, putting the British dreams of being the first to claim Mount Everest as their own, in serious jeopardy.

With the growing reputations of the German and American climbers, the British mountaineers knew that 1953 was perhaps their last chance to be the first to reach the summit of Mount Everest. The desperate desire for Everest glory led the authorities in Britain to transfer the leadership of the expedition from Eric Shipton—a veteran and much loved mountaineer, as well as the leader of the 1951 Everest Expedition—to the able shoulders of John Hunt. This was seen to be a necessary, if unpopular move. Hunt went about the mission with mechanical precision. His first task was to create a team of the strongest climbers, and for this he looked not just to Great Britain, but the entire Commonwealth.

Born just before the First British Everest Reconnaissance Expedition reached Mount Everest,

Overwhelmed by the adulation, Tenzing often joked about how far he had come from carrying loads on his back as a young Himalayan porter to flying high in airplanes. A year after the Everest climb, he opted for a gentler hike in the Rosenlaui valley near Meiringen in the canton of Berne, Switzerland.

Facing page: After climbing Everest, the next challenge for Hillary was to reach the South Pole, which he did successfully on 4 January 1958.

Edmund Hillary went to Auckland Grammar school and, after grudgingly attending two years of university, followed in his father's footsteps to become a professional beekeeper. Hillary was sixteen before he even saw a mountain and twenty before he climbed one. On a trip to the South Island of New Zealand, Hillary was staying with a friend at the famous tourist resort of The Hermitage when he saw two climbers who had returned from summiting Mount Cook, the highest mountain in the Southern Alps. He decided then and there that he too wanted to climb a mountain, and that too the very next day. That's how he found himself on the top of Mount Olivier, his first mountain. That was in 1939.

By 1951—with a break for the Second World War, where he served as a navigator for the RNZAF in the Pacific theatre—Hillary had graduated from the Southern Alps in New Zealand to the much hardier Alps of Europe and finally the treacherous and relatively unknown peaks of Himalayas. Before attempting to climb Mount Everest, Hillary had scaled 11 different peaks over the height of 20,000 feet (6096 m).

Hillary was a member of the 1951 British Expedition to Everest. During that expedition, the team managed to scale the Khumbu Icefall and enter the Western Cwm. Once on the mountain, they assessed that the route up to the South Col was feasible. They forged the new southern route up Everest and managed to get to the top of the Icefall before retreating. In the same year, Hillary ventured with three others to make six first ascents of peaks over 20,000 feet in the Garhwal Himalayas. He was also part of the 1952 expedition to Mount Cho Oyu, again under the leadership of Shipton. However, the

expedition failed to reach the summit. Hillary was back climbing the Alps when they both received their invitation by the Joint Himalayan Committee to join the 1953 Everest Expedition.

Tenzing, on the other hand, had a completely different trajectory of life. Born in Moyey village of Tibet in 1914, Tenzing was raised in Nepal and was a resident of India. For his community, the Sherpas, the mountain summits were sacred—they were the dwelling places of the Buddhist gods and were not to be violated by human presence. But despite his family's scepticism, all Tenzing had ever wanted to do was climb mountains. His first time on Mount Everest was as a high altitude

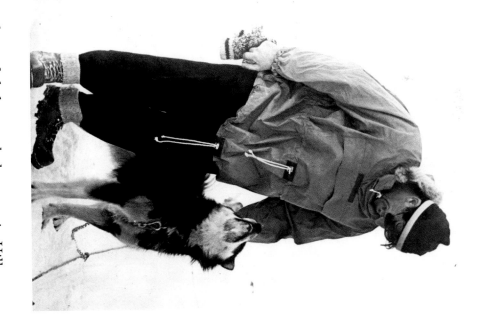

The lanky Hillary loved the mountains and was to later criticise the lack of sportsmanship and ethics in the increasingly commercial Everest expeditions. Seen here wearing his inimitable blue striped hat at Camp IV on Mount Everest.

Facing page: For a man who had never seen a mountain until the age of 16 and never climbed one until he was 20, Hillary's ascent of Everest less than a decade-and-a-half later was nothing short of remarkable.

Preceding pages: Seen here Sir Edmund Hillary and Tenzing Norgay in a moment of quiet camaraderie and celebration with mugs of hot tea at Camp IV in the Western Cwm after their successful ascent of Everest.

❝ It was 11.30 a.m. My first sensation was one of relief—relief that the long grind was over, that the summit had been reached before our oxygen supplies had dropped to a critical level; and relief that in the end the mountain had been kind to us in having a pleasantly rounded cone for its summit instead of a fearsome and unapproachable cornice. But mixed with relief was a vague sense of astonishment that I should have been the lucky one to attain the ambition of so many brave and determined climbers. It seemed difficult to grasp that we'd got there. I was too tired and too conscious of the long way down to safety really to feel any great elation.

But as the fact of our success thrust itself more clearly into my mind; I felt a quiet glow of satisfaction spread through my body—satisfaction less vociferous but more powerful than I had ever felt on a mountain top before. I turned and looked at Tenzing. Even beneath his oxygen mask and the icicles hanging from his hair, I could see his infectious grin of sheer delight. I held out my hand, and in silence we shook in good Anglo-Saxon fashion. But this was not enough for Tenzing, and impulsively he threw his arm around my shoulders and we thumped each other on the back in mutual congratulations. ❞

—**Edmund Hillary** describes what it felt **to reach the summit of Mount Everest**

porter in the 1935 Shipton-led Everest Expedition. Tenzing carried loads as a porter for the 1936 and 1938 expeditions too.

It would be 18 years and five failed tries before Tenzing finally made it to the top of Mount Everest. His first break came in 1947, when after undertaking a dramatic rescue during a Swiss expedition to the Himalayas, he was made a Sirdar (Sherpa leader) for the first time. In 1952, Tenzing was promoted to a full climbing partner by the Swiss Expedition to Everest, when he and veteran mountaineer Raymond Lambert came tantalisingly close to the summit of Everest.

As leader of the 1953 British attempt, it is believed that John Hunt wanted to include a

Sherpa as a part of the core climbing team to honour the Sherpas' contribution to the effort to scale Everest. Given his experience, prowess and reputation, Tenzing was Hunt's inevitable choice.

Leading from the front and with extreme precision, Hunt arrived with his team in March 1953. Trekking with 10 climbers, dozens of Sherpa guides and 350 porters carrying tons of equipment, the party finally arrived at Base Camp on 12 April 1953. Hunt immediately divided his team into small groups and sent them to foray into the mountain and get acclimatised. Despite meticulous planning and rigorous execution, the expedition was met with a number of obstacles. The first of which was the Khumbu Icefall, an

at Camp IV. Traversing the south face of Mount Lhotse, they reached the South Col on 21 May. It was this camp at a height of 25,900 feet which would be the staging ground for the final push for the summit.

Hunt had decided that only four climbers, in teams of two, were going to get a chance to make a summit bid. The partnerships were not predetermined, with Hunt wanting to observe the climbers and pair them according to their complementary strengths and personalities during the expedition. His final pairings: the first team to make the summit bid was to comprise Thomas Boudrillon and Charles Evans while the second team would be that of Hillary and Tenzing.

Commenting on his early impressions of Tenzing, Hillary recalls, "I had found Tenzing an admirable companion—capable, willing and extremely pleasant... although not perhaps technically outstanding in ice-craft, he was very strong and determined and an excellent acclimatiser. Best of all, as far as I was concerned, he was prepared to go fast and hard."

The first bid for the summit was made on the morning of 26 May. Boudrillon and Evans set out with their closed circuit oxygen equipment

ever-shifting river of ice with huge crevasses and frozen blocks of ice and rock. To Hillary, the Icefall looked more treacherous and vastly different than it had two years ago.

Establishing a route through the Icefall took almost two weeks and had to be kept open for a while to enable the large number of people and equipment to pass through to the next stage. By 1 May most of the party was on the Icefall or the Western Cwm, but bad weather slowed them all down. It had snowed every day for the last six weeks. Every morning the climbers awoke to find that their previous day's hard work undone by fresh snowfall. There were fears amongst the team that the monsoon that year had arrived early and that they would have no choice but to turn back.

But the team soldiered on. Two weeks later, by 14 May, most of the party had moved to live

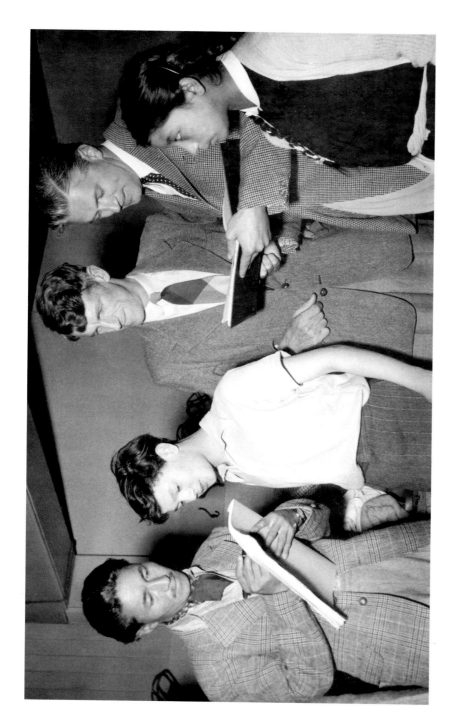

Hillary and Tenzing were the latest idols, their handsomeness only adding to their charm. Seen here on a visit to Beaconsfield Film Studios (England), autographing scripts.

Facing page: *Having realised the long-standing British dream of conquering Everest, expedition members arrived in London amidst much adulation and fanfare. Seen here is Tenzing, holding aloft the ice axe that he and Hillary used to get to the summit.*

and got to 300 feet (91 m) of the summit before bad weather and concerns about the remaining oxygen levels in their tanks forced them back.

The bad weather persisted for the next two days, delaying the second bid for the summit. Perched at a height of 27,900 feet (8503 m), Hillary and Tenzing woke at 4 a.m. on 29 May, hoping to get ready and set out in good time. They soon realised that Hillary's boots had frozen over and he had to spend the next two hours thawing them over a stove flame.

The pair finally set out from their high camp at 6.30 a.m., wearing, according to Hillary, "all the clothes we possessed—string singlet, woollen shirt, Shetland wool pullover, woollen underclothes, thick down trousers and jackets and over them all strong windproof trousers and jacket with a hood over the head. On our hands we had three pairs of gloves—first silk, then woollen, then windproof." On their backs were packs that, including their aluminium oxygen tanks, weighed 14 kilograms (over 30 lbs).

Generally regarded as the two fittest members of their team, 33-year-old Hillary and 39-year-old Tenzing had a daunting task ahead of them. Everyone before them had failed to climb that coveted summit. The questions that faced them were: Would they be able to make it? Would anyone be able to make it to the top of Mount Everest?

Climbing carefully and hopefully they reached the South Summit by 9 a.m. Recalls Tenzing:

"We look up. For weeks, for months, that is all we have done. Look up. And then there it is—the top of Everest. Only it is different now: so near, so close, only a little more than a thousand feet above us. It is no longer just a dream, a high dream in the sky, but a real and solid thing, a thing of rock and snow, that men can climb. We make ready, we will climb it. This time, with God's help, we will climb it on to the end."

But there was an obstacle. Hillary and Tenzing were faced with an almost vertical 40-foot high rocky spur, which seemed to stand imposingly between them and the summit. Later to be christened Hillary Step, this rocky face seemed insurmountable until Hillary found a crack in the wall and jammed his body partially

Hunt did not decide and declare the composition of the two final climbing teams till the very end, giving a chance for friendships to be forged and mutual trust to be developed. Seen here, Charles Wylie translating a letter to Tenzing and the cook Dawa Thondup.

Facing page: *Failure, it seemed, was not an option. Tenzing went prepared on his final summit bid, sure that he would have the opportunity to unfurl the flags tied to his ice axe.*

Following pages: *The 1953 expedition, much like the earlier ones, comprised a large party with hundreds of porters carrying tons of equipment up to Base Camp.*

into it, managing to wriggle up, with Tenzing following it, managing suit. Slowly Hillary began to cut small steps into this rock face with his ice-axe with no idea how long he would be at it. Finally the ridge dropped steeply away in a great corniced curve and Hillary saw that to his right "a slender snow ridge climbed up to a snowy dome about forty feet above our heads."

Talking about what they did next, Hillary later wrote, "It was too late to take risks now, I asked Tenzing to belay me strongly and I started cutting a cautious line of steps up the ridge. Peering from side to side and thrusting with my ice-axe, I tried to discover a possible cornice, but everything seemed solid and firm. I waved Tenzing up to me. A few more whacks of the ice-axe and a few very weary steps and we were on the summit of Everest."

Once on the summit, Tenzing took out his ice-axe and unfurled the attached flags of Britain, Nepal, United Nations, and India. He then went on to bury some sweets and a chocolate as a Buddhist offering to the gods, while Hillary placed a cross, given to him by Hunt, next to it. They spent 15 minutes on top of the summit. Hillary took the famous photo of Tenzing posing with his ice-axe. There are no photos of Hillary on top of the summit as Tenzing had never used

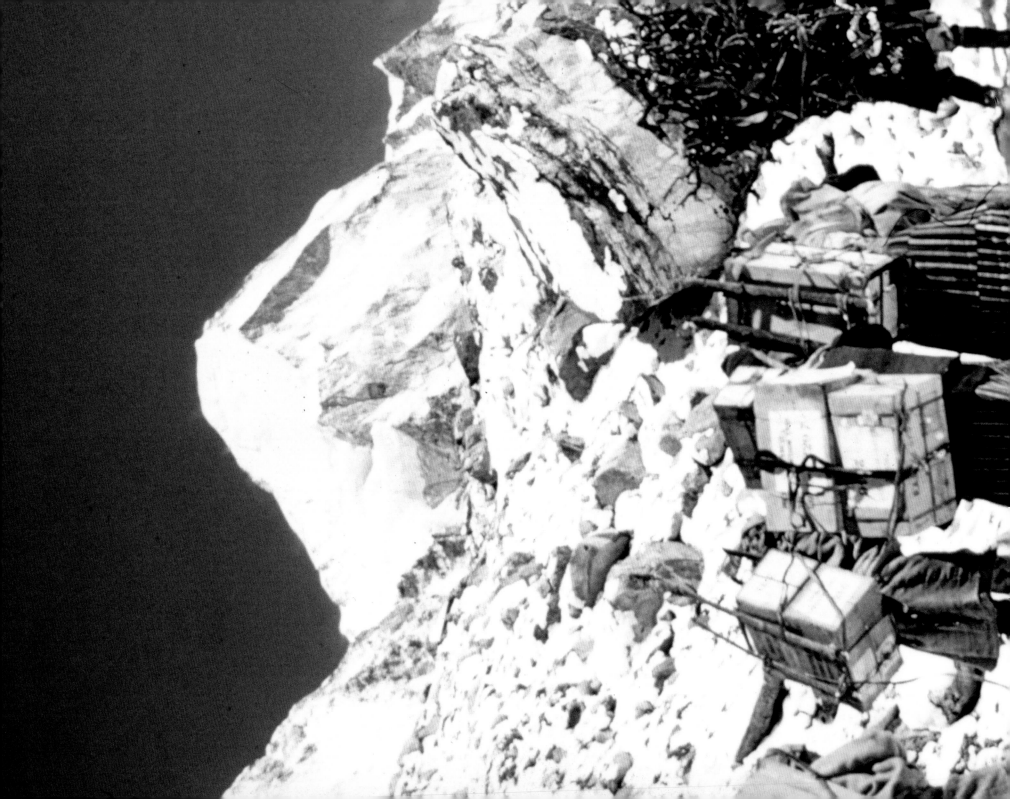

a camera before, and according to Hillary, he was not about to start teaching him on top of Mount Everest. They also took pictures of the view from the summit to prove that they had indeed been there. The two also looked around for any signs that Mallory and Irvine had been there but found nothing.

The news of their success reached the world on 2 June, the eve of the coronation of Queen Elizabeth II. While Hunt and Hillary were knighted, Tenzing was awarded the George Medal.

Many asked the question: Who had stepped on Everest first—Hillary or Tenzing? But for years they were met either with silence or the answer:

Both. Officially, Hillary, Tenzing and Hunt always maintained that the two men reached the top together. This was as much about camaraderie as it was about preventing any possible anti-colonial backlash. But several years later, Tenzing put a rest to all doubts and debates when, in his autobiography, he disclosed that Hillary was actually the first of the two to step on the summit.

After the feat at Everest, Tenzing went on to become a Director of Field Operations at the Himalayan Institute of Mountaineering in Darjeeling, India, where he led a quiet life till his death in May 1986. Sir Edmund went on to participate in an expedition across the Antarctica to the South Pole in 1958, but then chose to concentrate on setting up schools and hospitals in the Kathmandu region through his Himalayan Trust. He was also briefly, from 1984–1989, the New Zealand High Commissioner to India. Sir Edmund died at the age of 88 in January 2008.

By becoming the first men to stand atop the world's highest mountain, Hillary and Tenzing forever sealed their place in history. But over the years, it was their enduring humanity and legacies of goodwill that earned them a place forever in the hearts of people across the world. Not only did they pave the way for future conquests of Everest, but they also set the standard of sportsmanship by which each of them would be measured.

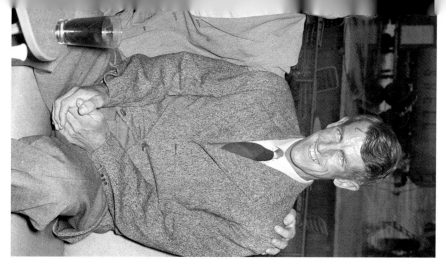

Facing page: *News of Hillary's and Tenzing's Everest success reached London on the eve of the coronation of Queen Elizabeth II. Hillary was appointed a Knight Commander of the Order of the British Empire while Tenzing was awarded the George Medal. Seen here, Queen Elizabeth II and Prince Philip, the Duke of Edinburgh, talking to Tenzing at Rashtrapati Bhavan, New Delhi, in 1961.*

Centre: *While Hillary and Tenzing were the ones who eventually became the first men to stand on top of Mount Everest, expedition leader John Hunt was instrumental in getting them there. Seen here together at Zurich airport in July 1953.*

Above: *Hillary and Tenzing's many honours included being awarded the Gurkha Dakshina Bahu and Nepal Tara respectively by King Tribhuvan of Nepal.*

CHAPTER 4

The Sherpa People
Unsung Heroes of
Himalayas

History: The Sherpas live in the high mountain region of eastern Himalayas and are believed to have migrated from Tibet to Nepal 500 years ago.

Culture: The Sherpa are Buddhists who traditionally believed that Chomolungma or Everest was the dwelling place of gods and prohibited human trespass. They were primarily traders who lived semi-nomadic lives; this changed when the expeditions to Everest began.

Renowned For: Their remarkable physiology that enables them to be more resilient to altitude sickness than others on extreme heights.

Some Famous Sherpas: Tenzing Norgay, Apa Sherpa, Ang Rita, Babu Chiri Sherpa

> **It has been a long road...** From a mountain coolie, a bearer of loads, to a wearer of a coat with rows of medals, who is carried about in planes and worries about income tax. **"**
>
> —**Tenzing Norgay Sherpa** reflecting on how much his life changed since he became the first person along with Sir Edmund Hillary to summit Mount Everest in May 1953.

The Sherpa or the "people of the East" migrated from Tibet to Nepal over 500 years ago. They first came to the world's attention when the earliest expeditions to Mount Everest hired them as porters. Seen here, a group of Sherpas on the South Col with Charles Wylie and Wilfred Noyce during the 1953 expedition.

The early military–style expeditions comprised a large number of explorers and mountaineers carrying tons of equipment and supplies with them, requiring, at times, hundreds of porters to carry all of it from camp to camp. See here, Sherpas carrying supplies to Everest Base Camp for the 1963 American expedition team.

Facing page: The Sherpa porters also double up as cooks during the expeditions. Though modern day climbers rely a lot more on dried foods, Sherpa diet consists of basic meals of either tsampa (roasted barley flour), potatoes, porridge or rice.

I t would be audacious to ask the question —Would Mount Everest have been scaled successfully when it was, or even at all, without the presence of the Sherpa people? It might be safe to conclude that without the participation of the Sherpa people, the early expeditions would have been less successful, more arduous and perhaps have had a higher mortality rate. It is undoubtedly the Sherpa people on whose backs the world's tallest mountain was conquered.

Literally the "people of the East", the Sherpas are believed to have migrated to Nepal from Tibet over 500 years ago, leading nomadic and semi-nomadic lives. A deeply spiritual people, the Sherpa revere the world's highest mountain—Chomolungma—as Goddess Mother of Earth. Swathed in pristine snow and plumes of white clouds, the mountain was considered holy ground and off limits to humans. But that was to change with the coming of Western mountaineers, who sought to tame and conquer Mount Everest, the latest frontier in geographical feats.

Now recognised and admired for their remarkable prowess and tenacity in high altitude climbing, the Sherpa people first came to the notice of the mountaineering community in the 1920s, when those in search of Everest glory hired them as local porters to carry tons of equipment required for the military-style expeditions of those days.

Renowned explorer and veteran Himalayan mountaineer Dr Alexander Kellas became the first person to note and record the near indispensability of the Sherpas to any high-altitude climbing expeditions in the region. It was

in the early 20th century that he took notice of the fact that their bodies acclimatised differently to that of others at extremely high altitudes, making them less susceptible to physiological deterioration associated with those heights.

Their stamina and unique mountaineering skills were noticed by George Leigh Mallory, too. After the 1922 expedition, he is said to have reported to a joint meeting of the Royal Geographical Society and the Alpine Club that the Sherpa could carry heavy loads up to heights of 25,500 feet, sometimes repeating the feat three days in a row. This fact alone is believed to have made possible the high camp method of climbing Everest that mountaineers employ to this day.

Described by the early Everest climbers as possessing an extremely positive attitude, and an exceptional resistance to cold, the Sherpa, while integral to the expeditions, were also

> The trail from Kathmandu to the foot of Everest winds for 185 miles [297 km] through the valleys and foothills of the Himalayas. These Himalayan expeditions are possible only because of the barefooted tribesmen, who were born to walk and walk to live. I feel there are many spirits carrying me along. 〉〉
>
> —Yuichiro Miura describing the Sherpa porters in his diary of the 1970 Everest Skiing Expedition

the first to perish on the icy slopes of the mountain. The first recorded deaths on the Everest are that of seven Sherpas who died in 1922 as a result of an avalanche that was inadvertently triggered by Mallory and his team when they made a second assault on the summit right after a snowfall.

Over the last 60 years, there have been several poignant stories of heroic feats of the Sherpa—in 1963, they carried three severely debilitated climbers for two days on their backs down to Namche Bazaar from Base Camp. Sadly, there are equally grim stories recounting where they were left to die, such as the case of the Nazi climbing team of 1939, which abandoned their Sherpa guides on Nanga Parbat after terrible weather conditions forced the expedition back.

Sometimes carrying up to three times their own weight on their diminutive frames, the Sherpas started out as load-bearing porters. Very soon, the stronger Sherpas became part of the higher altitude climbs and the actual summit bids. They were part of the core teams that mapped, planned and executed expeditions.

That one of the first people to stand on top of the world's highest mountain was Tenzing Norgay, a Sherpa, is only fitting. Today, they are very much the masters of their mountains (see *The Mountain, It Belongs to Us*, pages 104–105 and *Super Sherpa Apa*, pages 106–107).

Their remarkable physiological adaptability has been the subject of a number of studies. A 1976 study in the USA concluded that after living in one of the world's highest regions for several centuries, the Sherpas have undergone a process of genetic adaptation which gives them an advantage in high altitudes—they do not show the same physiological deterioration or the same propensity to altitude sickness as an average climber.

This adaptation has resulted in the presence of unique haemoglobin binding enzymes, hearts that utilise glucose, and lungs with an increased efficiency in low oxygen conditions. While physically less strong or able than their Caucasian counterparts living in relatively similar altitude conditions, it is this genetic adaptability combined with deep knowledge of the mountains and a mastering of some of the most demanding weather conditions that makes the Sherpa a "Super Climber".

The Sherpas are renowned for their unique genetic makeup which allows them to acclimatise in higher altitudes much faster than other climbers, making them indispensable to Everest expeditions. Seen here, Sherpas eating and resting at Camp IV during 1953.

Facing page: The remarkable Sherpas often carry up to three times their own body weight to great heights. Although they initially started out as load-bearing porters, soon the strongest and most skilled of them were promoted to being part of the actual climbing teams.

The Mountain, It Belongs to Us

Name: Babu Chiri Sherpa

Country of origin: Nepal

Age: 34 years

Everest feat: Spent a record 20 hours on the summit of Mount Everest

The Sherpa people may have started out as a footnote in the pages of Everest history—as native coolies of the European gentlemen climbers—but soon they were part of the main narrative and were equal expedition partners to record-seeking professional mountaineers. Then Tenzing Norgay Sherpa—who also started out as a load-bearing high altitude porter—created Everest history when he, along with Sir Edmund Hillary, became the first person to stand on the summit of the world's tallest mountain on 29 May 1953. Today, the Sherpa people write Everest history. The world records of some of the most interesting and challenging feats on Everest belong to the Sherpa people. The most famous of these are of course Tenzing Norgay and Apa Sherpa (see *Super Sherpa Apa*, page 107) who holds the record for the most number of successful ascents of Mount Everest.

Equally compelling are the feats of Nawang Gompu Sherpa, Babu Chiri Sherpa and Ang Rita Sherpa amongst others.

When Nawang Gompu climbed Mount Everest for the second time in May 1965, he became the first person in the world to summit the highest mountain twice.

Men of the mountains, some of the Sherpa men have set remarkable climbing records. Seen here (L to R) Apa Sherpa, who has summited Everest a remarkable 21 times, Ang Rita who has scaled the peak 10 times, each time without oxygen, and Babu Chiri, who spent the longest time on the summit itself: 20 hours.

Babu Chiri has more than one record to his credit. In 1995, he summited Mount Everest twice in two weeks. But his most remarkable achievement was when, after climbing the peak successfully, he stayed on the summit for a period of 20 hours—something thought impossible by many experts around the world. During the same climb, he also set the record for the fastest ascent by climbing in 16 hours and 56 minutes. A new record was set by Pemba Dorje in May 2004 when he scaled the mountain in 8 hours and 10 minutes.

Ang Rita Sherpa, also called Snow Leopard by some, climbed to the top of Mount Everest 10 times, and each time without oxygen. He started out at the age of 15 as a porter and made his first successful ascent on 7 May 1983. His last climb was in 1996, just 12 days after eight climbers died and several others were stranded in a storm, famously written about in the account by American journalist Jon Krakauer in his controversial account of the "Into Thin Air" incident.

Name: Ang Rita

Country of origin: Nepal

Age: 48 years for the final ascent

Everest feat: Scaled Mount Everest 10 times, each time without oxygen

ANG RITA SHERPA'S SUCCESSFUL CLIMBS

Date of Climb

1. 5 July 1983
2. 15 October 1984
3. 29 April 1985
4. 22 December 1987
5. 14 October 1988
6. 23 April 1990
7. 15 May 1992
8. 16 May 1993
9. 13 May 1995
10. 23 May 1996

Integral to expedition teams, the Sherpa have, over the years, also had a high number of fatalities. In fact, the first recorded deaths on the Everest were that of seven Sherpas who died as a result of a 1922 avalanche. Seen here, porters carrying ladders through an icefall on Everest.

Climbing Everest once is achievement enough, some have dared to come back a few more times, but Apa Sherpa has defied all belief to scale the mountain a record 21 times. Seen here during his 20th climb in 2010.

Super Sherpa Apa

Name: Apa Sherpa

Country of origin: Nepal

Age: 51 years for the final climb

Everest feat: Has scaled Mount Everest a record 21 times

C limbing Mount Everest once is an amazing feat. Climbing it 21 times in as many years is something else altogether. It is an achievement that makes people stop and look in awe, it goes down in record books, and becomes the feat to beat. Apa Sherpa, the man to scale the mountain more times than anyone else in the world, takes it in his stride. He knows it is special, he just doesn't seem to think it is extraordinary.

Like many Sherpas, Apa started out young. He began by working as a kitchen boy and porter in 1985, lugging the equipment of other climbers up and down several Himalayan peaks. He first climbed Mount Everest in 1990 and since then, this superstar of the climbing as well as the Sherpa community has reached the summit of Mount Everest almost every year, except 1996 and 2001, and twice in 1992.

His record-setting 21st climb on 11 May 2011, at the age of 51, was, according to him, his last. He does not plan to climb beyond the Base Camp in the future. Apa made the final ascent as part of the Eco Everest Expedition whose explicit objective was to clear the Everest of garbage.

For Apa, the mountain is Chomolungma, a sacred place, and he has expressed deep concerns about its degradation, often mentioning that when he had just started climbing, the Everest trail was covered in ice and snow and now it is dotted with bare rocks.

An iconic figure amongst the Sherpas, the now USA-based Apa set up the not-for-profit Apa Sherpa Foundation in 2009. The foundation aims to establish schools and create employment in Nepal.

APA SHERPA'S SUCCESSFUL CLIMBS

Date of Climb

1.   10 May 1990
2.   8 May 1991
3.   12 May 1992
4.   7 October 1992
5.   10 May 1993
6.   10 October 1994
7.   15 May 1995
8.   26 April 1997
9.   20 May 1998
10. 26 May 1999
11. 24 May 2000
12. 16 May 2002
13. 26 May 2003
14. 17 May 2004
15. 31 May 2005
16. 19 May 2006
17. 16 May 2007
18. 22 May 2008
19. 21 May 2009
20. 22 May 2010
21. 11 May 2011

CHAPTER 5

1970

Yuichiro Miura
The Man Who Skied Down Everest

Name: Yuichiro Miura

Age at Time of Ascent: 37 years

Country of Origin: Japan

Everest Feat: First person to ski down the slopes of Mount Everest

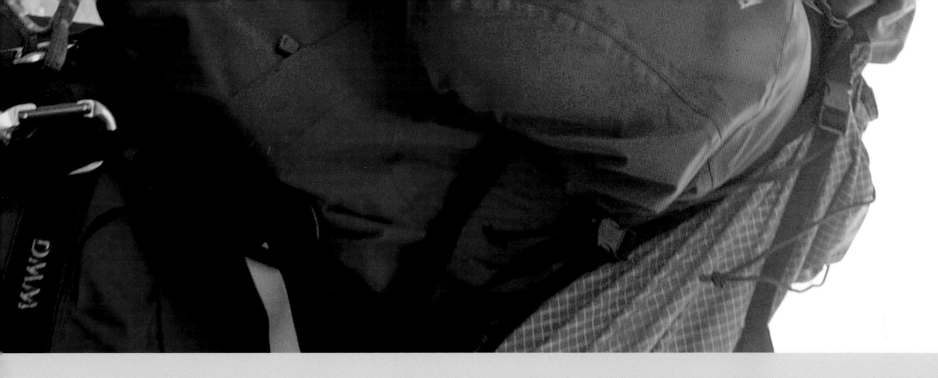

❝ *I am alive. They say I skied 6600 feet in 2 minutes and 20 seconds. I fell 1320 feet. I stopped 250 feet from the crevasse. Numbers have meaning in the world below. But in this almost airless world, what do they mean? Was it a success or a failure? That I am alive must be the will of some higher power.* **❞**

—**Yuichiro Miura's** diary after his 1970 Everest Skiing Expedition

Yuichiro Miura returned to Mount Everest, in 2003, 33 years after becoming the first man to ski down the slopes of the world's highest mountain, this time determined to make it all the way to the summit. Seen here with his son Gota praying at Base Camp.

Climbing with his 33-year-old son Gota Miura on 24 May 2003, 70-years and 223-days-old Miura became the oldest man to summit Mount Everest, beating the earlier record set by fellow Japanese climber Tomiyasu Ishikawa, who climbed the peak aged 65 years and 176 days. Father and son display their national flag after reaching the peak.

I n the last 60 years many men and women have successfully scaled Mount Everest, and in doing so a handful of them have set new records, earning for themselves a permanent place in history. In this exclusive and elite list of record holders, Yuichiro Miura's name stands out.

In 1970, Miura shocked the world and the climbing community by becoming the first person in the world to ski down the slopes of the world's highest mountain.

Born on 12 October 1932 in Aomori Prefecture, Japan, Miura is the son of the legendary skier Keizo Miura—the man who not only pioneered skiing in the Hakkoda-san mountains but also continued to ski down from some of the highest peaks in the world till the age of 100. Although Miura studied veterinary science at the University of Hokkaido, he could not escape the spirit of adventure and the love for skiing that seems to be embedded in his DNA.

Miura joined the International Ski Racers Association in 1962 and became the first Japanese professional skier to participate in international competitions. Two years later in 1964, he clocked 172.084 kilometres per hour to set a new record for speed skiing at the Kilometro Lanciato, or Flying Kilometre, in Italy. Although the record was broken the very next day, Miura was unconcerned. His real passion, he discovered, lay not in speed but high altitude skiing. "It seems to me that greater than the satisfaction of winning a competition is the joy of forgetting yourself and becoming one with the mountains," says Miura.

In the following years, Miura went on to ski down several slopes (see *No Slippery Slopes for*

75-year-old Miura was back at Mount Everest in 2008, determined to better his age record. He got to the top on 26 May 2008, only to realise that he had been beaten just 24 hours earlier by 76-year-old Nepalese Min Bahadur Sherchan.

Miura, page 116) including Japan's most sacred mountain and highest peak, Mount Fuji, and Australia's highest peak, Mount Kosciusko. Despite successful ski descents from some of the world's highest peaks, legend has it that Miura had not considered conquering Mount Everest till he met Sir Edmund Hillary. In New Zealand at the invitation of the country's Tourism Bureau, Miura had the opportunity to listen to

““ Am I really alive? I pounded with my hands and banged my head on the ice—I was living again—How dearly I felt that I was myself again! It is really good to be alive but the Everest of our dreams is still to be conquered. That elusive Everest of our dreams will be refined and polished in our hearts and minds, gleaming like the translucent air of the Himalayas where the true, the eternal, are elemental. That vision will be treasured however we grieve at the pollution of our hearts and minds by the sullied air and impurity of this murky nether world. In life, one event merges into the next. What is this Everest of our hearts? What was it that snatched me from the jaws of death, back to the world of man? I am a pilgrim again, to trudge the rest of my life toward the distant unknown, seeking this Everest, with this new lease of life granted to me. ””

—Yuichiro Miura reflecting on his miraculous escape from the Bergshrund Crevasse

Sir Edmund on the Everest Summit, after which he is said to have half-jokingly mentioned that he may consider skiing down Mount Everest. According to Miura, once Sir Edmund looked past the sheer audacity of the undertaking, he encouraged him to go right ahead and make history. This was in 1966.

Four years, many conversations and several requests later, the Nepalese government finally gave permission to Miura and his team to attempt this historical feat, but insisted that the route was to be down the South Col, almost 3000 feet short of the Everest Summit. The fact that he was not going to be allowed to ski down all the way from the summit did not bother Miura at all. He has, in fact, been quoted as saying, "My objective was clear, that was to ski down Everest… I did not really care about the summit at that time."

So it was that, in March 1970, Miura arrived in Kathmandu as part of the Japanese Everest Expedition. The expedition was not just an exercise in extreme skiing, it was a logistical undertaking of mammoth proportions. Miura notes in his diary, "It seems a simple idea to go to Mount Everest with a small group of enthusiastic skiers and climbers. But it is not simple. I wonder if I would have dared to think of this adventure if I'd known how complex it would be." It took 800 porters to carry 27 tons of equipment to the Everest Base Camp across a 185-mile (nearly 300 km) journey beginning in Kathmandu.

The ascent itself was challenging and fraught with extreme weather conditions. An icefall claimed the lives of six Sherpas in what is still considered by many to be one of the worst natural disaster accident in the history of Everest

Facing page: On 6 May 1970, the "Godfather of extreme skiing", 37-year-old Miura successfully skied down the slopes of Mount Everest, opening up the mountain to incredible sporting feats in the ensuing 40 years. Reaching speeds of up to 150-kmph, Miura narrowly escaped death when, after losing his balance, he stopped just metres short of falling into the Bergshrund Crevasse.

No Slippery Slopes for Miura

"To enjoy the world of skiing is one of the best pleasures mankind can have... It is more than a sport, it is the freedom of the universe."

—**Yuichiro Miura**

1964: Is the first Japanese national ever to compete in Kilometro Lanciato, Italy. He set the world skiing record of 179.084 kph

1966: Becomes the first person to ski down Mount Fuji. It was also the first time that Miura deployed a parachute to slow down his descent

1966: Skies down Australia's highest peak, Mount Kosciusko

1967: Skies down Mount McKinley, the highest peak in North America

1968: Becomes the first person to ski down Mexico's Mount Popocatepetoro

1969: Successfully skies down Chile's Towers of Paine

1970: Skies down Mount Everest from South Col, setting the world record of skiing down from the highest point on the earth

1981: Skies down Mount Kilimanjaro, the highest peak in Africa, with his 77-year-old father Keizo and his 11-year-old son Gota

1983: Skies down Mount Vinson Massif, the highest peak in Antarctica

1985: Skies down Mount Elbrus, Russia, the highest peak in Europe

1985: Skies down Mount Aconcagua, the highest peak in South America

2003: Summits Mount Everest successfully at the age of 70 years to become the oldest person to scale the mountain

2008: Summits Mount Everest again, this time at the age of 75 years

Facing page: *Miura is the son of the legendary Japanese skier Keizo Miura; father, son and grand-sons (Yuta and Gota) often ski together. The family is seen here on the slopes of the French Alps.*

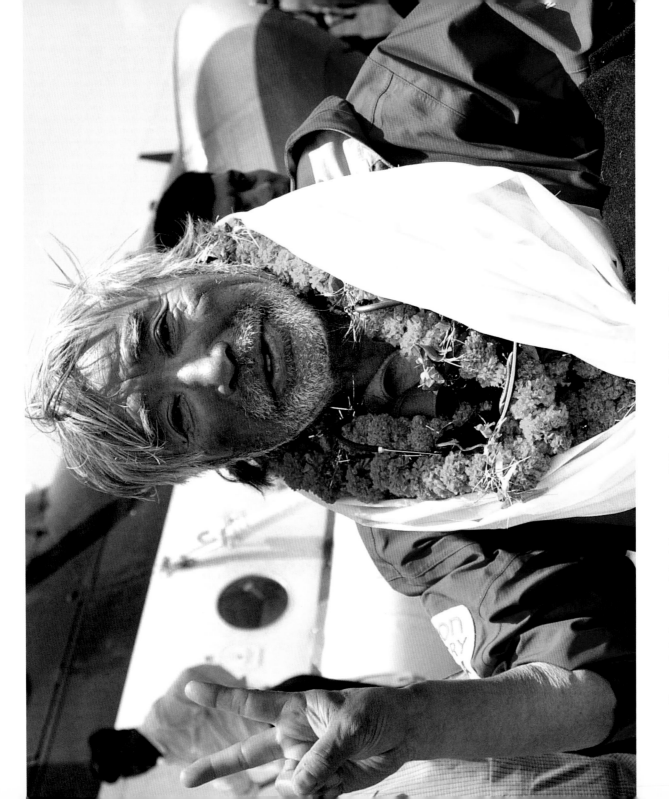

Miura was the first Japanese professional skier to participate in international competitions, but found that it was high altitude skiing that attracted him more.

Facing page: *The lightweight equipment used by today's skiers is light years away from what was used by Miura and his peers in the early 1970s.*

Following pages: *Father Keizo, son Yuichiro and grandson Yuta skied down the Valley Blanche, from Aiguille du Midi to Chamonix in the French Alps.*

expeditions. Five camps were set up, starting from the base and going all the way up, just above the Yellow Band on the South Col. The plan was to stay at each camp for some days to acclimatise their bodies gradually. As they set off from Camp IV their equipment weight was down to half a ton and their team had dwindled down to seven from the original 800.

On 6 May 1970, nearly two months after they first set off from Kathmandu, Miura did a short test run for a final check on his equipment. No one in the history of skiing or climbing had undertaken this feat before—in fact, no one in the world had skied over a height of 26,000 feet, neither had anyone deployed a parachute at this height. Miura had previously used a parachute while skiing down Mount Fuji to help slow his descent. But even the experts couldn't predict how the parachute would behave in the thin air. Even sky divers and astronauts open their parachutes at much lower heights than where he was planning to open his, notes Miura in his diary.

Wearing leather ski boots and a fighter pilot's helmet, with oxygen tanks and a parachute strapped to his back, Miura finally began his descent down the ice covered slopes of South Col just after 1 p.m. The historic feat, captured in the stunningly beautiful academy award winning documentary, *The Man Who Skied Down Everest*, shows that to slow his speed, Miura deployed his parachute almost immediately.

Despite serious reservations to the contrary, the parachute did

open at this height, but it failed to support Miura in his descent. It was in fact completely worthless, and the documentary captures Miura struggling unsuccessfully to control his speed and eventually losing his footing and sliding towards the Bergshrund Crevasse—the world's largest crevasse.

The documentary shows some of the sherpas averting their eyes from the horrific sight of Miura falling like a rag doll towards certain death. But Miura miraculously survived, as he hit a small patch of snow just 250 feet (around 60 m) from the edge of the crevasse.

A near-death experience on the icy unforgiving slopes of the world's highest mountain could easily lead normal men and women to hang up their boots and contemplate a life of quiet retirement. But men like Miura are rare. On being asked about this experience later, he reflected: "When I planned to ski Everest, the first thing I faced was 'How can I return alive?'... All the preparation and training was based on this question. But the more I prepared, the more I knew the chance of survival was very slim. Nobody in the world had done this before, so I told myself that I must face death. Otherwise, I am not eligible."

Admired by many across the world, Miura has been hailed by some as the godfather of extreme skiing. However, over the years, some critics have questioned the credibility of his feat and the claim of being the first man to ski down Mount Everest, citing that he did not do so from the summit (see *Trailblazing Descents*, page 122). Miura

Trailblazing Descents

Name: Davorin "Davo" Karničar

Country of Origin: Slovenia

Age at Time of Ascent: 38 years

Everest Feat: First man to ski down from the summit of Mount Everest

Yuichiro Miura's name is etched permanently in the annals of Mount Everest's history as the first person to ski down its slopes; however it will not be as the man who did so all the way down from the summit. That feat belongs to Slovenian Davorin "Davo" Karničar. In 2000, the 38-year-old Karničar became the first person to complete an uninterrupted ski descent all the way from the summit to the base camp, taking the South-East Ridge Route.

An earlier attempt was made in 1996 by renowned Italian mountaineer Hans Kammerlander. However, he only succeeded in skiing down the North side of Everest in parts as there were areas of sheer rock that just could not be skied around. He had to remove his skis and walk part of the way. During that attempt he did, however, set a speed record of 16 hours and 45 minutes to climb from the Base Camp to the summit of Everest via the North Col. Coincidentally, Karničar also made his first attempt the same year, but after losing his index and little fingers to frostbite in a snowstorm, he had to abandon the whole exercise.

The year after Karničar's successful ski descent saw the first snowboard descent from the summit.

Slovenian Davo Karničar bettered Miura's feat by becoming the first person to ski non-stop from the summit of Mount Everest to the Base Camp on 7 October 2000.

On 22 May 2001, Austrian snowboarder Stefan Gatt climbed all the way to the summit of Mount Everest and began his descent from a height of over 28,800 feet (8535 m). But after descending around 500 feet (152 m) he chose to walk from there to 25,000 feet (7620 m), citing safety reasons. From there he rode down to 21,000 feet (6400 m). His feat was topped a mere 24 hours later by 22-year-old Marco Siffredi, who began his descent from the summit down the Norton Coloir North face and continued down a two-hour ride to just below 21,000 feet. A year later, during his second attempt at snowboarding down Everest, Siffredi mysteriously disappeared from a height of 27,800 feet (8473 m), where his tracks came to an abrupt halt.

Previous page: *Hans Kammerlander, who has climbed 13 of the world's 14 tallest mountains, attempted to better Miura's record by skiing down right from the summit of Everest. However, he had to take his skis off after 300 metres because of safety issues.*

Above: *The Miura men are easily the "First Family" of skiing in Japan. Keizo and Yuichiro are legendary in what they have achieved, and Gota represented Japan in Freestyle Mogul skiing at the 1994 Lillehammer and 1998 Nagano Winter Olympics. The three generations of adventurers skied down western Europe's highest mountain, Mont Blanc, in February 2003 to celebrate Keizo Miura's 99th birthday.*

Following pages: *On 23 May 2001, 22-year-old Marco Siffredi took extreme descents down Mount Everest to a new level by becoming the first person to snowboard uninterrupted from the summit to just below 21,000 feet (6400 m).*

remains undeterred by such debates. In the 15 years following the ski descent down South Col, he went on to successfully ski down from the highest peaks in seven continents (see *No Slippery Slopes for Miura*, page 116) including Mount Kilimanjaro in 1981, where he was joined by his 77-year-old father and 11-year-old son, Gota.

In the early 1990s, Miura faced a slew of health problems and retired from high altitude skiing. He was diagnosed with a metabolic syndrome and then with arrhythmia and atrial fibrillation. Meanwhile, his father Keizo and son Gota were still skiing—and doing so successfully. Gota had gone on to represent Japan in Freestyle Mogul skiing at the 1994 Lillehammer and 1998 Nagano Winter Olympics.

Inspired by their spirit and success, Miura determined to get into shape and scale the summit of Mount Everest—something that he had failed to accomplish in 1970. As part of the preparation to scale Everest, Miura successfully climbed Goyo Peak in 2000, Mera Peak in 2001 and Mount Cho Oyu in 2002. In 2003, 33 years after he first set foot on it, Miura returned to Mount Everest.

This time he climbed all the way to the top. In doing so at the age of 70 years and 223 days, he became the oldest person to reach the summit of Mount Everest. This record was broken four years later in 2007 by another Japanese climber—Katsusuke Yanagisawa who reached the peak at the age of 71 years. The very next year Miura returned again—after undergoing two operations for catheter ablation—to summit Mount Everest on 26 May 2008, this time at the age of 75 and reclaiming the title of the oldest person to reach the summit, only to lose it within days to a Nepalese man, Min Bahadur Sherchan, after the latter produced birth records to show that he was indeed 76 years old when he scaled the summit a barely 24 hours before Miura.

Now, five years and a broken pelvis later, the 80-year-old Miura has announced that he will once again attempt to scale the iconic mountain, this time from the Chinese side. For men like Miura, the adventure never stops. "I want to show that you don't have to throw away your dreams and ambitions when you hit 80. Eighty is the new 60."

> " Every step seems to rob us of our breath. It is an effort to walk, to talk, even to think. It is almost too much of an effort to live. As we climb our bodies have been acclimatised—the chest cavities increase to take in more air, the red blood corpuscles multiply to absorb more of the available oxygen. But here, with half the level of oxygen at sea level, it is beyond human acclimitisation. Survival is a matter of sheer endurance. The brain requires twenty times more oxygen than the muscles for normal functioning and at this altitude it begins to deteriorate. Intellect and senses are dulled and therefore one can be in danger without realising it. A long stay would be fatal. "
>
> **—Yuichiro Miura writing in his diary after reaching the height of 18,000 feet in April 1970**

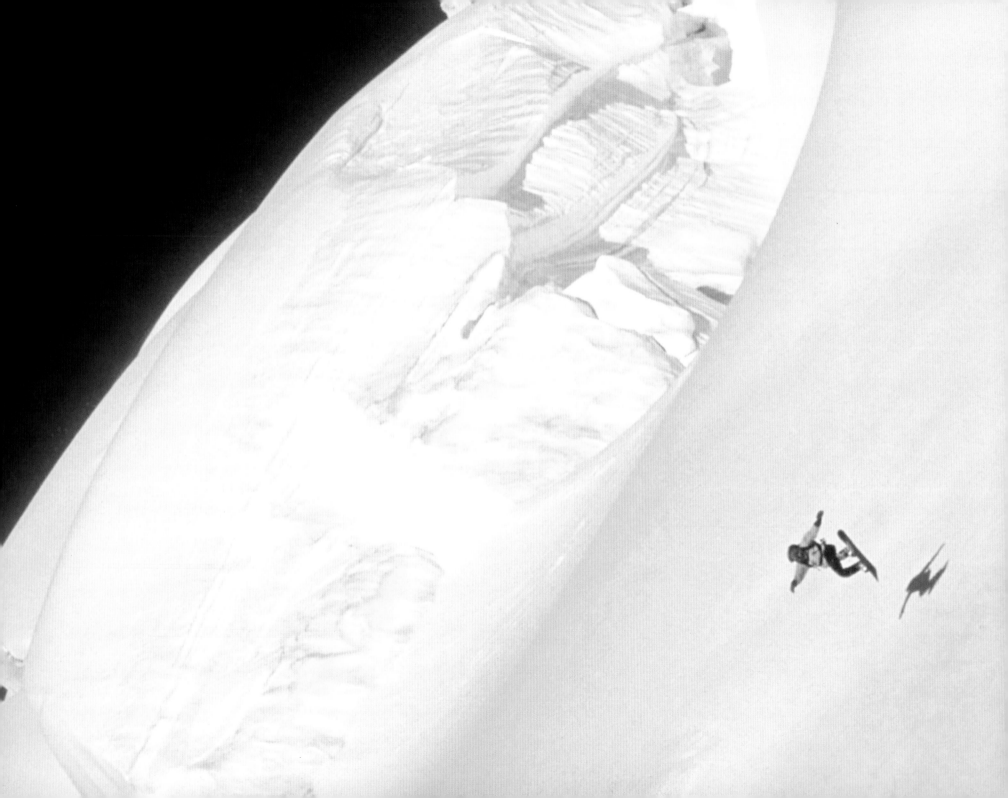

CHAPTER 6

1975

Junko Tabei

To Boldly Go Where No Woman Has Gone Before

Name: Junko Tabei

Age at Time of Ascent: 35 years

Country of Origin: Japan

Everest Feat: The first woman to summit Mount Everest

❝ Technique and ability alone do not get you to the top—it is the will power that is the most important. This will power you cannot buy with money or be given by others—it rises from your heart. **❞**

—Junko Tabei

On 16 May 1975, 35-year-old Junko Tabei from Japan overcame deeply entrenched gender discrimination in her country to become the first woman to stand on the summit of Mount Everest.

What made Tabei's historic ascent even more remarkable was that just twelve days earlier, she and her entire expedition party had been buried under a heavy avalanche. Tabei is seen here with Nepal's Sirdar Ang Tsering who pulled her out of the snow and then accompanied her up to the summit.

"I can't understand why men make all this fuss about Everest... It's only a mountain," Junko Tabei is believed to have said after climbing right to the top of the Mount Everest.

But there was some serious fuss to be made about Tabei's Everest ascent. Only 36 people had stood on Mount Everest's summit before Tabei; all of them men. On 16 May 1975, defying stereotypes and battling prejudices, Tabei created history by becoming the first woman to stand on the peak of the world's highest mountain.

Born on 23 May 1939 in a small town in North Japan, Tabei was one of seven children. A very frail child, she suffered from weak lungs and was never very athletic. In fact, often being teased for being too "sickly", Tabei shunned sports.

When she was 10 years old, Tabei tagged along with a teacher on a school climbing trip to Mount Asahi (6,233 feet/1900 m) and Mount Chausu (6,365 feet/1940 m), in Nasu. This outing was to change Tabei's life forever—she fell in love with climbing. It was a non-competitive sporting pursuit that suited her temperament. She could climb at her own pace, reaching the top even if she was slow, could quit, turn around and return another day and the mountain peak would still be hers to claim.

Since, at that time, mountaineering was not considered to be an appropriate occupation for women in Japan, Tabei went on to graduate with a degree in English literature from the Showa Women's University. Tabei became very serious about mountain climbing soon after graduation and took it up professionally. At the age of 30, she formed the Ladies Climbing Club (LCC) of Japan in 1969.

Only 4 feet and 9 inches tall, the diminutive Tabei had soon scaled most of the Japanese peaks, including Mount Fuji, and was looking for bigger mountains to climb. On 19 May 1970 she, along with members of her club, scaled Annapurna III and now they set their sights on Mount Everest.

The club applied to the Nepalese government for a permit in 1971, but the climbing schedule was full for the next four years. This was when Japan's Nihon Television and the Yomiuri Shimbun newspaper came to her rescue. 1975 was declared the International Women's Year by the United Nations, and to mark the occasion, the two organisations decided to sponsor an all-women expedition to Mount Everest. Tabei was one of the fifteen women chosen from hundreds of candidates.

After an intense training period, Tabei left her two-and-half-year-old daughter at home and headed to Kathmandu with the rest of the team.

Making good progress, the all-women expedition, along with their Sherpa guides were spending time getting acclimatised at 20,669 feet (6,300 m) when they were hit by a terrible avalanche on 4 May. All climbers, their tents, climbing equipment and the Sherpas were buried under a thick blanket of snow. The Sherpa guides did a remarkable job of rescuing everyone. Tabei was pulled out from under the snow by the legs by her Sherpa Ang Tshering, who later accompanied her to the summit.

Tabei was covered in welts and bruises and her legs and back hurt. However, despite this, after making sure that everyone was alive and alright, Tabei, as deputy expedition leader, decided to continue further up the icy slopes of Everest. From here on, the climb was a challenge for a

Wonder Women

When Junko Tabei made history as the first woman to summit Mount Everest, she directed the spotlight on other women mountaineers. While there are several women out there climbing mountain after mountain successfully, there are two of them who stand out for what they have achieved.

The first of them is Wanda Rutkiewicz, who made history on 16 October 1978 by becoming the third woman in the world and the first European woman to reach the summit of Everest. The first woman to scale 8 of the 14 peaks over 8000 metres high, Rutkiewicz is regarded by many as the greatest woman climber ever.

Born in 1943 in Plungiany, then a part of Poland, Rutkiewicz climbed solo to the summit of some of the world's biggest mountains, often without oxygen. After Everest, Rutkiewicz conquered the Nanga Parbat in 1985 and in the very next year she became the first woman to ever summit the perilous K2. Over the next five years she scaled five peaks of over 8000 m, namely— Shisha Pangma in 1987, Gasherbrum II in 1989, Gasherbrum I in 1990 and summited both Cho Oyu as well as Annapurna I in 1991. Rutkiewicz's remarkable achievements also include a second ascent of the North Buttress of the Eiger (after

Messner and Habeler), and the ascent of the North Face of the Matterhorn in winter and the South Face of Aconcagua.

In 1992, she tragically disappeared near the summit of Kanchenjunga after attempting to scale it via the southwest face route. It is not known if she made it to the summit. If she did, not only would it have been her 9th peak over 8000 m, it would also have made her the first female to ever summit all three highest mountains in the world.

The second remarkable woman mountaineer is the English climber Alison Hargreaves. On 13 May 1995, the 33-year-old climber became the first woman to reach the summit of Everest without supplementary oxygen and unassisted by Sherpas. Hargreaves first came to the world's attention in 1993 as the first climber to solo in all the great north faces of the Alps in a single season, including the formidable north face of the Eiger.

In 1995, Hargreaves went on to accomplish the unprecedented feat of reaching the summits of both Everest and K2 without oxygen in the same summer. However, on her way down from K2, Hargreaves met with a blizzard and perished on the slopes on 13 August, ending the promise of greater achievements to come.

The first woman on Everest, Tabei (extreme right) was part of the May 2003 Golden Jubilee Celebration of the conquest of Mount Everest by Edmund Hillary and Tenzing Norgay. Seen here in Kathmandu (from L to R) with Tashi Tenzing (Tenzing's grandson), Jamling Tenzin Norgay (Tenzing's son), Pemba Doma Sherpa (first Nepalese woman to summit Everest via the North Face), Reinhold Messner's girlfriend Sabine Stehle and Messner.

Facing page: *Seen here crampons, which are traction devices necessary to travel securely on snow and ice, including walking on glaciers and climbing icy slopes.*

battered Tabei. But determined to get to the very top, Tabei soldiered on, often crawling on her hands and knees.

Twelve days later, 35-year-old Tabei's perseverance was justly rewarded, when she became the first woman to successfully summit Mount Everest. Had she and her team been delayed by the avalanche the record could easily have slipped through Tabei's fingers. For, just 11 days later, 37-year-old Phantog, a Tibetan member of the Second Chinese team to ascend Mount Everest, became the second woman to summit the mountain.

Fighting for the social equality of women in Japan, Tabei is believed to have said that climbing Everest was easier than overcoming discrimination in Japan. At that time, women were discouraged from indulging in non-family related pursuits. However, since Tabei's remarkable achievement, there have been several Japanese women climbers who have gone on to scale Everest, among other mountains. The list includes Tamae Watanabe, who holds the record for being the oldest woman to have climbed Everest, not once but twice.

After conquering Everest, Tabei went on to become the first woman to complete the Seven Summits when she scaled the 16,023 foot-high (4883 m) Carstensz Pyramid in 1992.

Tabei returns to the mountains time and again, because they teach her "a lot of things", making her realise, "how trivial my personal problems are". Tabei likes to describe herself as "a free spirit of the mountains".

Now over 70, Tabei shows no signs of slowing down. Her dream is to climb the highest mountain in every country. With over 60 of them already scaled, she has just over two-thirds of the way still to go. And when she is not climbing mountains, Tabei spends time as the director of the Himalayan Adventure Trust of Japan, an organisation dedicated to preserving mountain environments.

CHAPTER 7

1978 & 1980

Reinhold Messner

Climbing Alone and Without Oxygen

Name: Reinhold Messner

Age at Time of Ascent: 34 years

Country of Origin: Italy

Everest Feat: The first person
(along with Peter Habeler) to summit Mount Everest
without oxygen equipment and then the first person
to summit it solo two years later

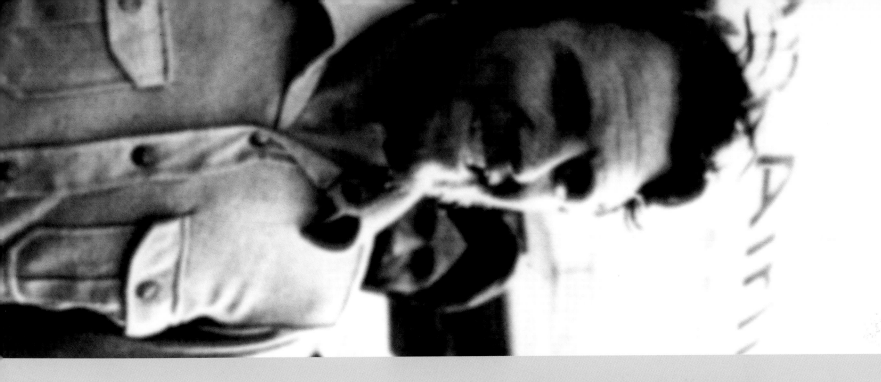

❝ *When we proposed climbing Everest without oxygen in 1978, people told us it wasn't possible, that we were risking our lives. They said we would lose our brains up there. When the first climbers on the Austrian expedition we joined came down, they said we shouldn't even try. It was hard: I didn't know if I'd have a chance to go back to Everest, and Everest is Everest. I was determined then to try and get as high as possible.* **❞**

—**Reinhold Messner** in an interview on 30 March 2003

Reinhold Messner and Peter Habeler turned conventional mountaineering wisdom on its head on 21 May 1978 by becoming the first men to climb to the summit of Mount Everest without using supplemental oxygen.

Always testing the limits of his own endurance, Messner walked 1700 miles (2735 km) across Antarctica in 1989. Fifteen years later, at the age of 60 he traversed 1200 miles of the Gobi Desert on foot. Seen here, showing nomad children his GPS watch on the outskirts of the Gobi Desert in Mongolia.

Facing page: *Even though it has been decades since Messner last climbed a famous mountain peak, he continues to be a towering figure in the climbing community. Seen here at a press conference at the Smíchov Climbing Festival, 20 November 2009, Prague, Czech Republic.*

Reinhold Messner is unquestionably one of the greatest mountaineers of all times. Some would even call him a living legend. In his over three thousand climbs he has time and again turned conventional mountaineering wisdom on its head and redefined the limits of what is "possible"—and never more so on 8 May 1978 when he, along with Peter Habeler, became the first person to complete the successful ascent of Mount Everest without any supplemental oxygen. Two years later, while the world was still talking about this extraordinary feat, Messner went right ahead and astonished it even more—this time by becoming the first person to summit the world's highest mountain solo—and without supplemental oxygen.

Messner, who in 1986 went on to become the first person to summit every one of the 14 mountains over the height of 26,246 feet (8000 m), has been climbing since the age of five. Born in the South Tyrol region of Italy, Messner says he took to climbing because of two reasons: first, his father was a climber and encouraged his sons to follow suit, and second was just a lack of any alternative sport in the region during his growing years. The rock towers of Geislerspitzen were his and his brothers' playground and it was here that they began mastering freestyle rock climbing.

Messner and his younger brother Günther became climbing partners and were soon scaling mountains in the Dolomites and the Alps, where they gained experience as high altitude mountaineers. By the time Messner was 20 and Günther 18, they had climbed some of the hardest routes in the Dolomites and Western Alps. The opportunity for their first Himalayan

climb came in 1970 when both brothers (Messner, 26 and Günther, 24) signed up for an expedition to the ninth-highest peak in the world, Pakistan's 26,660 foot (8125 m) Nanga Parbat, led by Karl Herrligkoffer.

That expedition was to change Messner's life forever.

Climbing from the Rupal face of the mountain, the expedition was plagued by bad weather from the beginning. Despite this, Messner was given an opportunity to make a bid for the summit alone. Well on his way up, he was surprised to find his brother Günther following him. Günther was meant to be at Base Camp preparing ropes so that the other climbers could follow suit. Messner waited for him to catch up and then went on to summit the peak along with his younger brother.

However, once on top, the weather conditions and Günther's increased exhaustion and altitude sickness made it impossible for them

Described by writer John Krakauer as the "Michael Jordan" of mountaineering, in 1980 Messner followed his "sans oxygen" ascent of Everest by becoming the first person to summit the mountain solo. He climbed alone without any Sherpa guides, teammates or oxygen supplies. Seen here, Messner recounting his climb for an audience.

Facing page: *Perhaps the most flamboyant of all climbers, Messner enjoys the good life, including spending time at his summer home, the 13th-century Juval Castle in south Tyrol. Seen here taking a lesson in far eastern cuisine in a Munich restaurant, before his expedition to Tibet.*

Following pages (144-145): *In 2000, Messner, along with American climber Conrad Anker and British mountaineer Stephen Venables, followed Sir Ernest Shackleton's 1916 route across the remote island of South Georgia in the southern Atlantic Ocean. Seen here, Messner and Anker being blasted by the morning winds on the Fortuna Glacier, South Georgia.*

to return to their camp before dark. It was at that moment that Reinhold took a fateful judgement call. Dismissing the descent down Rupal face as too steep for Günther, he decided that their only option was to descend via the other side of the mountain, the treacherous Diamir face. It was a risky and controversial decision as a descent via the Diamir face had not been achieved previously.

Although the weather conditions improved on their way down, Günther's health did not. After spending another night on the mountain, Messner instructed Günther to wait and went ahead to scout for the best route down. Moments later, Günther was swept away by

a small avalanche and was not found despite Messner's arduous search. Messner's account was disputed by a number of mountaineers who blamed his ambitious nature for Günther's death.

It was not until 2005, when Günther's body was found roughly where Messner had said he had disappeared, that his version of the incident was vindicated.

Out of this tragedy was born what finally became Messner's trademark style of climbing.

An emotionally broken Messner lost seven toes and three fingertips to frostbite during the expedition. He knew his days as an elite

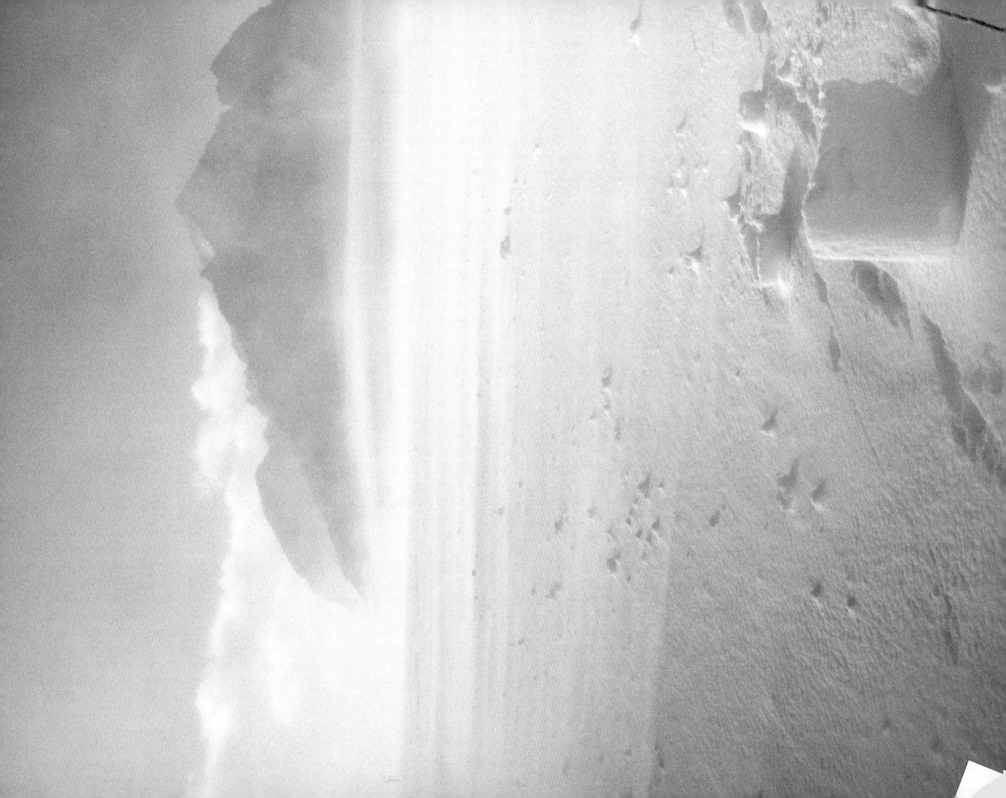

From one legend to another: Italian sailor Giovanni, who has sailed across the world alone and won several prestigious races, in conversation with Messner, perhaps the greatest mountaineer of all time, in 1999.

rock climber were over and his entire focus now shifted to high altitude mountaineering. Günther's loss on his first Himalayan expedition was soon followed by the loss of two companions on Messner's second Himalayan foray, leading him to resolve that he would never again climb in large groups.

Messner found a kindred spirit in Austrian mountaineer Peter Habeler. They had been climbing together since 1969 after meeting by chance while climbing in South America.

In 1974, together they climbed the north face of the Eiger in 10 hours, nearly halving the previous record of 20 hours. Soon after, the two announced that they were going to attack an 8,000 metre (over 26,000 feet) mountain "Alpine style". Now Messner decided that he would climb the Himalayas as he had done the Alps—they would leave the Base Camp with a rucksack, scale the mountain as fast as possible before descending, and would always climb by "fair means", which excluded the use of supplemental oxygen. There would be no preparation along the route.

The idea was revolutionary. In the 1970s, all mountaineering expeditions carried huge amounts of oxygen for use above 8,000 metres

Despite hundreds of ascents under his belt, Messner has always prepared diligently for each new climbing expedition. Seen here during a training session at Plateau Rosa, Cervinia, Italy in 1989.

Stages of My Life

Reinhold Messner is perhaps the climbing world's most flamboyant personality. His life includes achievements as varied as solo ascents of some of the world's highest mountains, crossing the Arctic, completing a 1242 mile (2,000 km) expedition through the Gobi desert, setting up museums and serving a term as a member of the European Parliament. While simply reading through his expansive list of accomplishments may leave an ordinary person breathless, for Messner all these feats are simply categorised and compartmentalised according to which stage of life he is at, making it all seem a bit more manageable. He has publicly shared what he describes as the six stages of his existence:

Stage 1: The Vertical Life—an elite rock climber scaling the mountains of Dolomites and Alps
Stage 2: The High Altitude Life—high altitude mountaineering and scaling the peaks of Himalayas, including Mount Everest, without oxygen, and often alone
Stage 3: The Horizontal Life—exploration of vast, desolate landscapes like the Arctic and the Gobi desert

Stage 4: The Exploration of Holy Mountains and Myths—Messner set off on a quest to find the legendary creature of the Himalayas, the Yeti. He claimed to have seen it, describing it as the elusive Himalayan brown bear, earning

himself derision and notoriety in the process.
Stage 5: The Politician's life—his time as a member of the European Parliament
Stage 6: Retirement and setting up the Messner Mountain Museums

Messner is a man of many facets or avatars. Besides being a rock climber, an explorer, a mountaineer, he has also served a five-year term (1999–2004) as a Member of the European parliament and is a prolific author. Seen here, presenting his book Mi vida al limite *(My Life at the Limit) in Madrid, Spain in 2005.*

or what is termed as the Death Zone—so-called because it is at this altitude that most human bodies lose all ability to acclimatise, resulting in a slow deterioration of the body and a permanent brain damage. The longer a climber stays at this altitude, the more likely the occurrence of illnesses such as high altitude cerebral oedema and high altitude pulmonary oedema.

In 1975, Messner and Habeler scaled the 26,470 feet (8,068 m) high Hidden Peak summit of Gasherbrum I, without any of the trappings of traditional high-altitude climbing—porters, camps, fixed ropes, and oxygen, and thus set a whole new standard of mountaineering.

But the ultimate test of their method would be the ascent of Everest. In 1978, the Austrian Alpine Club agreed to allow Messner and Habeler to accompany their Everest expedition as an independent two-man team. The climb was to be from the South Col.

On 6 May 1978, Messner and Habeler set out from Everest's Camp II. Within 48 hours they were trudging through the snow up the Southeast Ridge toward the summit. Messner is famously quoted as later describing feeling as though he

Messner is seen here with another Italian adventure sports legend Giovanni Soldini. While Messner has climbed some of the world's tallest mountains alone, Soldini has sailed across the world solo.

permanent brain damage, Messner and Habeler stood atop the world's highest mountain, breathing nothing but the fresh and dangerously thin air. It was 8 May 1978. The world of mountaineering would never be the same again.

But Messner was not done yet. For the purist in him, scaling Everest without oxygen only served to pave the way for the ultimate feat—climbing the world's highest mountain solo. Messner's first solo climb of a peak over 8,000 m was that of Nanga Parbat, the world's ninth highest peak, in 1980. Messner then managed to obtain a permit for a solo climb from Everest's North Face, the Tibetan-Chinese Side. With only the mandatory Chinese liaison officer, an interpreter and his then girlfriend, Nena Holguin for company, Messner set up a single-tent advanced base camp at 21,325 feet (6,500 m). The two Chinese escorts remained at a lower camp while Messner and his girlfriend trekked between the two camps for a month. Messner set out for the summit on the morning of 18 August, when he once again created Everest history. Recalls Messner, "Climbing Everest solo without bottled oxygen in 1980 was the hardest thing I've done. I was alone up there, completely alone. I fell down a crevasse at night and almost gave up. Only because I had this fantasy—because for two years I had been pregnant with this fantasy of soloing Everest— was I able to continue."

After almost single-handedly revolutionising the world of high altitude climbing, today Messner lives a relatively quiet life with his family in his summer home of Schloss Juval, a 13th-century castle in the mountains of South Tyrol, Italy.

were "nothing more than a single narrow, gasping lung, floating over the mists and summits" during his final push for the summit.

Proving wrong the experts who had described their mission as impossible and predicted at worse their deaths and at best

Messner holding the boot belonging to his younger brother, who perished on Nanga Parbat in 1985. Many had held Messner responsible for 24-year-old Gunther's death. The discovery of his brother's body in 2005, in the vicinity of the place he had always maintained, vindicated his version and exonerated Messner of any responsibility.

Facing page: *Kammerlander proved to be an ideal partner for a tempestuous Messner. Together they achieved some of the most remarkable climbs, including the traverse Gasherbrum I and II (1984) in a single push and the northwest ascent of Annapurna (1985). Seen here together in Askole, Pakistan in 1985.*

CHAPTER 8

1998

Tom Whittaker

On a Prosthetic and
a Prayer

Name: Tom Whittaker

Age at Time of Ascent: 49 years

Country of Origin: United Kingdom/
United States of America

Everest Feat: The first disabled person to
summit Mount Everest

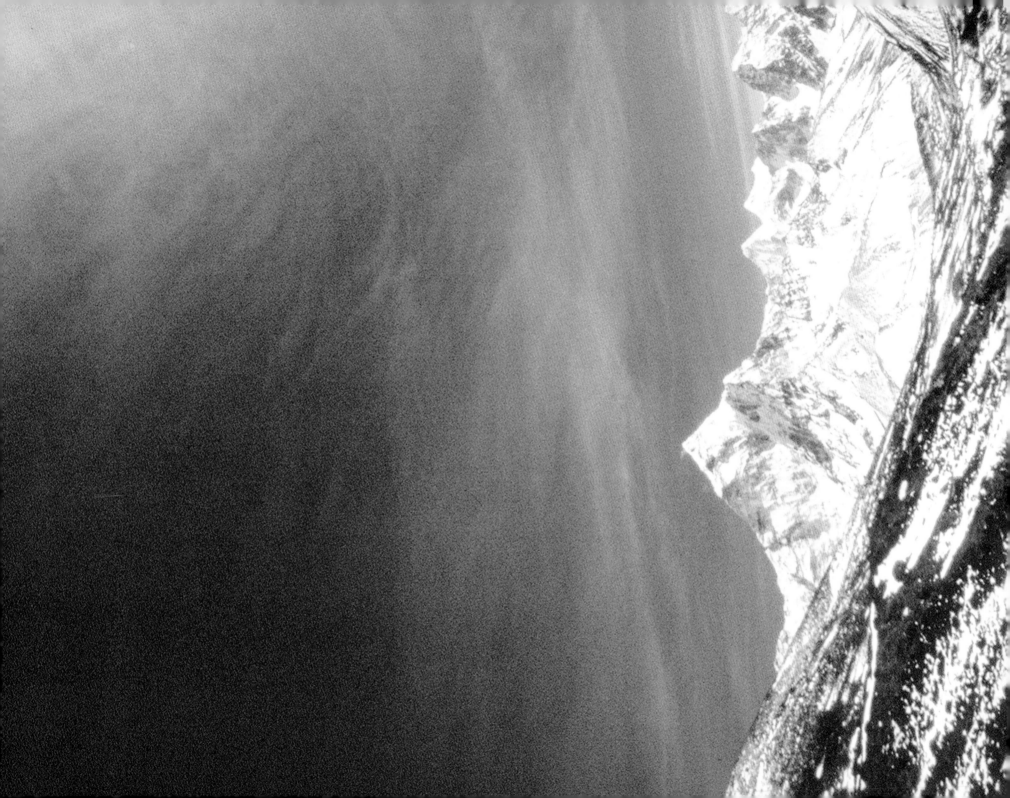

❝ Assaulted by the elements, in rarefied air, mountaineers do battle with giants of geography. In wind and snow, on rock and ice, they toil upwards. It has no intrinsic purpose; it is of no earthly good. There is no one to watch, no adoring public, no accolades. Financially it is often ruinous. Why then do we do it? The spirit of mountaineering is the need to sustain the soul through adventure. It is not the summit, it is the journey to the summit that is the prize. The outer journey leads us within. The rewards are in self-knowledge that comes from pursuing our dreams with love and courage. **❞**

—**Tom Whittaker** after successfully completing the ascent to Mount Everest in 1998

Having had to turn back twice before, Tom Whittaker returned to Everest in 1998 determined to make it all the way to the summit on his third attempt, in the process becoming the first disabled person to do so.

In 1998 Whittaker was accompanied by a group of disabled climbers from Cooperative Wilderness Handicapped Outdoor Group (CWHOG) founded by him in 1981. Seen here are Carla Tustak (who has cerebral palsy) and Whittaker.

Facing page: *Losing his right foot and kneecap in a car accident on Thanksgiving Day in 1979 changed 31-year-old Whittaker's life forever. Resolute to not let his disability limit him, he was kayaking just seven months later.*

In 1995, in his Everest Challenge summary report, a disheartened Tom Whittaker wrote, "The expedition failed to meet this objective, of placing the first disabled person on the summit of Mount Everest."

Whittaker could not have known that just three years later he would be writing a very different summary report—a report documenting a feat that would forever secure his place in the history of mountaineering. For, on 27 May 1998, just shy of his 50th birthday, Tom Whittaker became the first disabled person to plant his feet—one real, one prosthetic—firmly on the summit of Mount Everest.

This was his third attempt at scaling the mountain. In his first attempt in 1989, Whittaker climbed to 24,000 feet (7315 m) from the South Col route before he was forced back down by a raging storm that killed six people. In his second attempt, in 1995, Whittaker ascended from the rocky North Ridge route and reached a height of 27,500 feet (8382 m), becoming the first disabled person to climb above 25,000 feet (7620 m). However, just 1500 feet (457 m) short of the summit, Whittaker was forced to turn back after he realised that his oxygen supplies would not last the rest of the climb.

This achievement, while pathbreaking, was not enough for Whittaker. He was determined to come back and scale the remaining distance to the summit.

It was during this second attempt that fellow climber and teammate, Greg Child, gave Whittaker a stone, saying, "I picked this up on the summit and I want you to put it back where I got it from." And three years later, Whittaker did just that. He returned the stone to its rightful

place on the "roof of the world", a place he had pledged to stand on almost two decades ago.

His story begins in 1979. It was on a cold and wintry Thanksgiving Day that 31-year-old Whittaker's life changed forever. Whittaker's vehicle was met head-on by a car whose driver had lost complete control. The accident left Whittaker in a critical condition with multiple fractures. When he awoke from the emergency surgery, Whittaker realised that the accident had resulted in the removal of his right kneecap and the amputation of his right foot. For Whittaker, an athlete with ambitions of becoming a professional mountaineer, this was devastating. In a documentary Whittaker recalls, "The doctors put my knees back together as best as

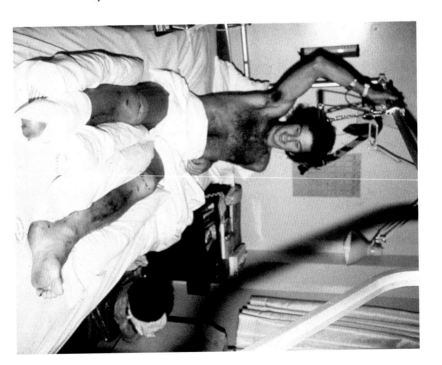

The climb to the top was challenging for Whittaker and he fell extremely sick at the high camp. Seen here on the fixed lines of the Lhotse Face.

> " Just yesterday Andy and I were singly focussed on the summit; today we would settle for our lives... Thus far in the spring of 1989, seven climbers had perished. Everest was wracking up some grizzly statistics, and still the storm raged."
>
> "The weather had deteriorated in the last two hours. Now a decision had to be made between staying or going. Either alternative could prove fatal. To do nothing and die in the mountain's clasp was not an option. Despite our fatigue, we went on. In normal conditions, we could make it to the food, shelter and our loved ones at Base Camp in two hours. Today it would be a crap shoot at best."
>
> "I am a Zombie. An amputee has to exert 35% more energy than someone with both feet. My prosthesis designed for ascending rock and ice is small and sinks deeper into the snow pack. The exertion has rubbed my stump raw and the discomfort in both knees, damaged in the same car accident that took my right foot, had gone from a dull roar to a temple pounding scream. And hour after hour the punishment continues. The three head-lamps that still functioned, searched the vast jumble of ice for clues. Then at last we saw faint pinpricks of wavering light, and like shipwrecked mariners, we embrace the men that have risked their lives to look for us. "
>
> —Vignettes from Whittaker's diaries (dated 1996, seven years after his first attempt)

they could and were saying that, at best, I would be good for pushing a grocery cart around a store but I certainly would not be doing any more mountaineering."

But Whittaker was not about to surrender his true passion simply because the doctors told him so. He was resolute. He was going to go kayaking, trekking, and he was going to climb mountains again. The first sport he returned to was kayaking, since that did not require the use of his lower leg. This was just seven months after the accident.

In the early days of rehabilitation, Whittaker faced a lot of social barriers, with people doubting his ability to participate in outdoor adventure activities. However, of the firm belief that "physical disability does not mean inability," Whittaker carried on his training. He also founded the Cooperative Wilderness Handicapped Outdoor Group (CWHOG) in 1981. The group's explicit aim was to create a platform through which people with disabilities could pursue recreational and adventure opportunities while cultivating a strong sense of self-esteem. Members of the CWHOG were to finally accompany Whittaker to Everest on his record-breaking expedition of 1998.

Ten years after the horrific accident, Whittaker was invited to join an expedition to Everest. His only condition—not to be treated as a prop or a marketing gimmick, but a full-fledged expedition member who would

The All Abilities Trek

Two years after he lost his right leg and knee cap in a horrific car accident, Tom Whittaker created the Cooperative Wilderness Handicapped Outdoor Group (CWHOG) at Idaho State University and directed the programme for 10 years. Its genesis was rooted in the negative social attitudes that Whittaker himself faced after his accident, and the organisation aims to provide recreational opportunities for disabled people while building up their self-esteem.

When Whittaker was planning his 1998 Everest Expedition, he invited members of the CWHOG to join him in the trek to Mount Everest Base Camp—the thought took many of the members by complete surprise. Once the astonishment wore off, however, a sense of immense purpose took over the group. Those who finally decided to make the trek christened the undertaking the All Abilities Trek.

The reactions to the trek ranged from polite scepticism to outright outrage.

According to Tom McCurdy, a member of the All Abilities Trek, "Many of our family members, friends and colleagues thought we were a bit loopy for attempting this challenging HOG trip; many people discouraged us from the very beginning. You see, we were planning on getting five people with disabilities, three of us in wheelchairs, into the Mount Everest Base Camp... We had the experience of running into another group of trekkers in Kathmandu who thought we should not be trying the journey either, a group from Norway or Finland who thought we had a death wish."

The team of the All Abilities Trek comprised twelve people in total, seven able-bodied and five disabled members. The five disabled members were Kyle Packer and Carla Yustak who have cerebral palsy, Steve DeRoche who is a double amputee below knees, Ike Gayfield, with transverse myelitis, and Tom McCrudy who is a paraplegic. Along the way, a passionate discussion over how to pronounce Khumbu led

to them calling themselves "Kripples in the Kumboo".

Defying the naysayers, the team finally made it to the Everest Base Camp, at a height of 17,600 feet, on 11 May 1998 and continued there for a three-night stay. They had successfully made the 21-day trek from Lukla in Nepal, demolishing all stereotypes about people with disabilities all along the way. Those who could, walked the whole way, while those who used wheelchairs made their way on horses and yaks.

Summing up the successful expedition, Steve DeRoche says, "The HOGs trekked to Everest Base Camp in support of Tom Whittaker's third Everest expedition. Everyone made it. Tom became the first disabled person to stand on the top of the world. Jeff Rhoads became the first person to summit twice in one week. Tom, Ike, and Kyle were the first wheelchairs in Base Camp. Lizzie Whittaker (Tom Whittaker's daughter), was the youngest at six to be a yak driver and walk the whole way there. Myself, a double amputee, was also a first to Base Camp. No one got sick, or hurt and nobody died."

Members of the All Abilities Trek at Namche Bazaar, in 1998. Front Row: L to R: Nathan Barsetti, Ali Orton, Tom McCurdy, Lizzy Whittaker (sitting on Tindy–Sirdar's knee), Cindy DeRoche, Cindy Whittaker, Kyle Packer. Back Row: L to R: Steve DeRoche, Bob Myers, Ike Gayfield, Jeff Brandt, Carla Yustak.

Facing page: *Members of the All Abilities Trek which accompanied Whittaker defied all skepticism and made it to Everest Base Camp successfully.*

> ❝ Plans are great because they endure till the first minute you engage the mountain and then everything is out of the window and then you basically have to live from day to day and you are continually rearranging what you have to do based on weather conditions, human conditions, the logistics of what you are trying to do on the mountain and so on. There are tons of variables and they are working sometimes in harmony but most often against one another and so you have lots of balls in the air at the same time and it is not like juggling balls; it is more like juggling a refrigerator, a chain saw and a bunch of other things. ❞
>
> —Tom Whittaker on the challenges and risks in attempting the ascent to Everest

undertake the entire climb. He trained hard and he trained well. Unfortunately, he was not to complete the ascent in 1989 and returned home, having barely survived.

By the time the 1995 expedition materialised, Whittaker was father to three-year-old Lizzie, whom he carried in a pack on his back up the Little Granite Mountain (one of the steepest peaks near his hometown, Prescott, Arizona) to train for the physical demands of the Everest ascent.

The final and successful expedition in 1998 was conceptualised, fund-raised and led by Whittaker himself. This time however, he had two other clear elements besides the main objective of successfully placing the first disabled person on the summit of Mount Everest.

The first of these elements was the All Abilities Trek, wherein a group of five people with

serious physical disabilities and seven able-bodied climbers would trek to the Everest Base Camp. The five disabled members of the team were drawn from CWHIOG and included Kyle Packer and Carla Yustak who suffer from cerebral palsy, Steve DeRoche who is a double amputee below the knees, and Ike Gayffeld and Tom McCrudy who are paraplegics (see *The All Abilities Trek*, pages 160-161). This feat not only challenged conventional wisdom about who can and should attempt to scale Mount Everest but also went a long way in breaking stereotypes about the capabilities of people with physical disabilities. Tom Whittaker's wife, Cindy, took on the responsibility of this aspect of the expedition.

The second element of the expedition was the Environmental Restoration Project, which wanted to point out the climbers' responsibility towards the very mountain that they seek to conquer. Aimed at cleaning up Mount Everest, the goal of this project was to retrieve 100 oxygen bottles and a ton of garbage from the high camps on the mountain. In all, they retrieved 89 bottles of oxygen in addition to the 59 they

Facing page: *Whittaker described his ascent to the summit as a "climb of imagination, technology and human spirit". Determined to succeed, he conceptualised, fund-raised and led the expedition himself.*

A Man and His Incredible Feat

Name: Mark Joseph Inglis

Country of Origin: New Zealand

Age at Time of Ascent: 46 years

Everest Feat: First double amputee to summit Mount Everest

Christmas Day 1982. Mark Inglis, a professional mountaineer, woke up in a hospital bed and looked down at his legs. The sheet seemed to end somewhere halfway down the bed. A devastated Inglis realised that he had just lost both his legs below the knee. Besides not being able to perform a hundred other everyday mundane tasks, Inglis could no longer do the one thing that he loved above all—climb mountains. Or so everyone around him thought.

Inglis was to prove them all wrong. And he was to do that not in a small measure but by undertaking the grandest of adventures. Twenty-four years after his amputation, on 15 May 2006, Inglis planted both his custom-made ultra-light carbon fibre prosthetic limbs firmly on the soft snow of the Mount Everest Summit. On that fateful day, Inglis became the first double amputee in the world to stand on the highest point on Earth—a place that few able bodied men and women dare to venture.

For Inglis, it was something that he just had to do. "The main thing is to always know that nothing in life is too hard. You never know until you give it a go."

Scaling Everest was a boyhood dream for

Inglis; his accident only temporarily placing it on the backburner. Climbing since the age of 12, Inglis was most at home in the mountains. In 1979, he began work as a professional mountaineer as a search and rescue mountaineer for Aoraki/ Mount Cook National Park.

In November 1982, while attempting to scale Mount Cook, the highest peak in New Zealand, he and his climbing partner Philip Doole were caught in a terrible blizzard and took refuge inside a tiny cave, which they nicknamed Hotel Middle Peak. Continued bad weather hampered rescue missions. After 14 days, Inglis and Doole were found inside the cave, barely alive. They had suffered severe frostbite, which resulted in Inglis's legs being amputated just below the knee.

Describing what happened on Mount Cook as a "hiccup", Inglis was back on a mountain in under a month. He says, "To be a mountaineer you have to have a couple of extra self-confidence genes otherwise you wouldn't want to be a mountaineer anyway."

In 1998 Inglis, a biochemistry graduate, collaborated with Wayne Alexander involved with the pioneering Britten Motorcycle Company to develop specialised ultra-light carbon fibre limbs for cycle racing. They continue to work together till today to develop a range of specialised artificial limbs.

It was this partnership that enabled Inglis to win a cycling silver medal at the 2000 Sydney Paralympics. Standing on the podium, receiving his medal, Inglis decided that it was time to revisit

*After losing both his legs below the knee in 1982,
professional mountaineer Mark Inglis went on to
become the first double amputee to summit
Mount Everest.*

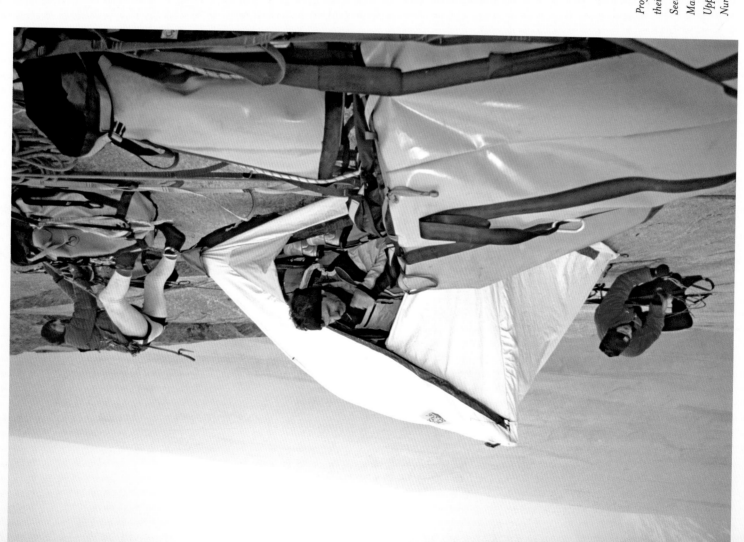

Professional mountaineers scale many mountains in their lifetime, but claiming Everest is always special. Seen here, climbers Jon Catto, Greg Child and Mark Synnot set up a hanging portaledge camp at Upper Headwall, Great Sail Peak, Baffin Island in Nunavut, Canada.

Mount Cook, the place he had first attempted to climb as a young man of 22. On January 2002, close to 20 years after he was found trapped on its icy slopes, Inglis successfully reached the top of Mount Cook. His climb has been captured in the compelling documentary, *No Mean Feat: The Mark Inglis Story*.

Standing atop the roof of New Zealand, Inglis decided it was time to go after his boyhood dream and attempt to stand on top of the roof of the world—the summit of Mount Everest. In preparation of this daunting task, Inglis first endeavoured to scale Mount Cho Oyu in Tibet. He did so successfully on 27 September 2004, his 45th birthday.

A confident and optimistic Inglis arrived in Nepal in early 2006. After a small mishap right in the beginning, the climb was smooth—while acclimatising at 21,000 feet (6,400 m) a fixed line anchor failed and Inglis fell and broke one of his carbon fibre prosthetic limbs in half; temporary repairs were made using duct tape while a spare was brought up from Base Camp.

After a total climb of 40 days, Inglis finally made it to the top of Everest, fulfilling a lifelong dream and proving that nothing is beyond the realm of possibility.

However, his moment of glory was shadowed by two dark clouds.

On the way Inglis had a massive hematoma from the constant pounding of the stump against the prosthetic limb. On his return, Inglis had to undergo yet another surgery where some more bone around his knees had to be trimmed. He also lost some fingertips to frostbite.

This physical discomfort was far easier to deal with than the psychological implications of the second incident. Inglis was roundly criticised by international media as well as members of the climbing community when it was found that he had walked passed a dying climber on his way to the summit. David Sharp, a British climber, was oxygen deprived and suffering from severe hypothermia and was found about 984 feet (300 m) below the summit. He died later.

Inglis has said that there was nothing that he could do. He explains that he was in the Death Zone, over 26,250 feet (8000 m) above sea level, where physical and intellectual strengths are hugely compromised. A later documentary showed that members of Inglis's team saw Sharp on the way down, when their oxygen supplies were low and many were suffering from frostbite. Some members also tried to help him, but Sharp was unable to even stand alone or walk leaning on anyone. Inglis has expressed confusion and frustration at being singled out by the media as he was one of 39 other climbers who passed Sharp that day.

Despite this criticism, Inglis continues to carry on with his charity work, which includes setting up and running Limbs4All which supports Kathmandu's spinal injury Rehabilitation Centre by providing them with specialist rough country wheelchairs. He is also a patron of the Cambodia Trust NZ, which provides prosthetic limbs to those needing them in Cambodia.

Today, Inglis is a motivational speaker and a wine maker and continues to search for adventures that help him redefine the limits of possibility.

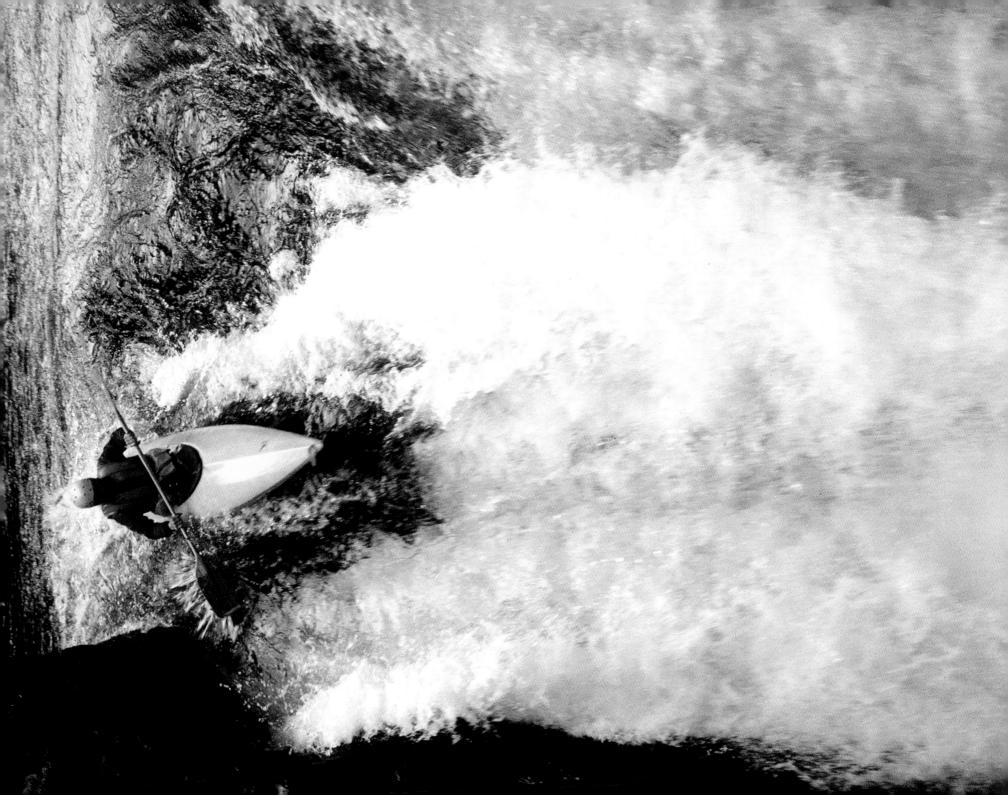

had themselves used and 1000 pounds (nearly 500 kg) of garbage from Camp II. Interestingly, the group received no financial support from Corporate America and financed it entirely out of its own pockets, including raising funds by selling autographed oxygen bottles for $350 each.

Both these objectives only accentuate the uniqueness and poignancy of Whittaker's personal success. Instead of deterring Whittaker, the two failed attempts only seemed to reinforce his resolve to scale Mount Everest. For his third attempt he trained tirelessly on the mountain itself for two months.

Despite extremely high levels of preparedness, there were several moments when it appeared that Whittaker's last chance to scale the mountain may not materialise after all, putting his Everest dreams to rest forever. Accompanied by his fellow climbers Angela Hawse and Gareth Richards, Whittaker made it up to a height of 27,000 feet before falling very sick.

In an article for the American Alpine News (October 1998), Angela Hawse notes that on 20 May 1998, at a height of 27,000 feet, Whittaker had to abandon his summit attempt because he showed symptoms of pulmonary oedema.

This happened because there were mixed reports about the weather and Whittaker tried to compress his climb into two days and pushed himself too hard.

In his final Ester-C Everest Challenge Report 1998 he explains: "We received regular weather forecasts, however, this ended up being a mixed blessing. The tropical storm that was predicted to put large quantities of snow on the mountain on 20 May never materialised. This forecast squeezed a large number of people into a small window of opportunity on 19 May. The congestion and confusion that ensued was the factor that led Angela, Gareth, and Tommy Heinrich to end their summit bid on the South Summit. It was also the factor that forced me to compress four days' climbing into two and start my summit bid on the night of my second day's travel from Base Camp. As we now know, the storm never materialised and a ridge of high pressure bathed the mountain for eight days."

Whittaker's condition improved with adequate medication and rest and he resolved to make one last effort to fulfil his two-decade-old dream, one day before his climbing permit was to expire.

He undertook the final assault in the middle of the night, and at 2 a.m., with more than half of humanity fast asleep, Whittaker finally stood on top of the world—literally, metaphorically, and very proudly.

For Whittaker, scaling Mount Everest has been a "climb of imagination, technology and human spirit" and seems to have been only the beginning of a record-setting adventure. He is aiming to become the first amputee to conquer the highest peak on each of the seven continents.

Facing page: *Individuals like Whittaker don't stop when they achieve a dream; they go on to dream bigger, more magnificent ones. Seen here is Whittaker kayaking through the rapids despite losing a leg in a car accident.*

Following pages: *The 1998 Everest Summit Team and All Abilities Trekkers each fulfilled their set objective—Whittaker became the first disabled person to summit the world's highest mountain and the All Abilities Trekkers successfully made the 21-day trek from Lukla in Nepal to the Everest Base Camp, spending three days there.*

CHAPTER 9

2001

Erik Weihenmayer
Blind Faith

Name: Erik Weihenmayer

Age at Time of Ascent: 41 years

Country of Origin: United States of America

Everest Feat: The first blind person in the world to summit Mount Everest

> **❝** *Twenty years ago when I went blind, it was tough to even find the bathroom. Now that I've climbed Mount Everest, well, I guess I've come a long way.* **❞**
>
> —**Erik Weihenmayer**

On 25 May 2001, American mountaineer Erik Weihenmayer redefined the rules of Everest climbing by becoming the first blind person in the world to reach the summit of Mount Everest.

Weihenmayer first contemplated scaling Everest after a chance meeting with geophysicist Pasquale Scaturro in 1999. Their expedition received a sponsorship of USD 250,000 from the National Federation of the Blind, USA.

Facing page: *The initial phase of climbing proved to be exceptionally challenging for Weihenmayer, with many, including the expedition leader, beginning to question his ability to make it to the top. But a determined Weihenmayer made it right to the summit.*

On 25 May 2001, American climber Erik Weihenmayer took carefully balanced baby steps to complete the precarious trek across the 656-feet-long (200 m) knife-edge ridge that leads to the Hillary Step—the final hurdle before the summit of Everest. With vertical drops of 10,000 feet (3048 m) and 7,000 feet (2133 m) into Tibet and Nepal on either side, it is a stretch that only about one tenth of all those attempting to scale Everest manage to cross. As ice and rock chipped off beneath his feet, Weihenmayer kept an ear open for the tinkling of bells tied on the packs of his climbing partners, walking just ahead. That was the only way Weihenmayer, who has been blind since the age of 13, could be sure that he was on the right track.

Taking his final step to stand on the summit of Mount Everest, Weihenmayer created history by becoming the first blind person to scale the world's tallest mountain. Defying naysayers' predictions of doom and exceeding his own expectations, Weihenmayer then went on to complete the ascents on all Seven Summits—the highest mountains on each of the seven continents—before he was 33 years old.

Born on 13 September 1968 with limited vision, Weihenmayer was unable to see straight ahead beyond a few feet and had to rely on his peripheral vision. He was suffering from a retina disease called retinoschisis, which meant that his vision would deteriorate slowly and would be gone completely by his early teens. For a young Weihenmayer, this was devastating. He initially refused to accept his blindness, rejecting all aids such as white canes and braille. Unable to participate in sports such as football and baseball, Weihenmayer began living on the margins of life at school.

That was until he discovered wrestling in high school. It was a sport where the importance of sense of touch far outweighed that of sight. Soon Weihenmayer was surprising his coaches, peers and even himself with his prowess and agility on the wrestling mat, pinning down opponent after opponent. He was 16 years old when he went to attend a camp for the disabled in New Hampshire. It was here that he was introduced to rock climbing—where the sense of touch triumphed once again.

Weihenmayer threw himself into sports, constantly pushing boundaries of what he could achieve as a person without sight. His love for mountain climbing grew when, after the death of his mother, his father took him and his brothers climbing

Weihenmayer spent two nights at Camp I; his progress was steady but slow. He had to keep his ears open at all times to listen to the tinkling of the bells tied to the packs of his climbing partners for guidance.

Facing page: *Trust, an important factor in any Everest expedition was absolutely indispensable in Weihenmayer's case. The climbing party consisted of mountaineering veterans as well as some of his closest friends. Weihenmayer had to rely completely on his teammates who would shout out the necessary instructions and warnings to help him make his way up the mountain safely.*

through the mountains of Spain, Peru, Pakistan and Papua New Guinea.

Meanwhile, he graduated high school and went on to study at Boston College and then became a teacher and wrestling coach at an elementary school in Phoenix, Arizona, where he began climbing the surrounding hills with partners who soon became friends. The climbing partners decided to venture further and began

training for an ascent of Mount McKinley in Alaska, the highest peak in North America. After scaling that in 1995 he went on to summit Mount Kilimanjaro in Tanzania in 1997.

Weihenmayer had not seriously contemplated climbing Mount Everest until a chance meeting with Pasquale Scaturro at a trade show in Salt Lake City, Utah in 1999. A leading geophysicist, Scaturro had been on a number of Everest expeditions and summited it successfully. He asked Weihenmayer if he had thought about climbing Mount Everest and when the latter replied in the negative, Scaturro immediately offered to put together an expedition that would help Weihenmayer get to the very top of the world's highest mountain.

Armed with a $250,000 sponsorship from the National Federation of the Blind, the two of them put together a team that comprised a mix of

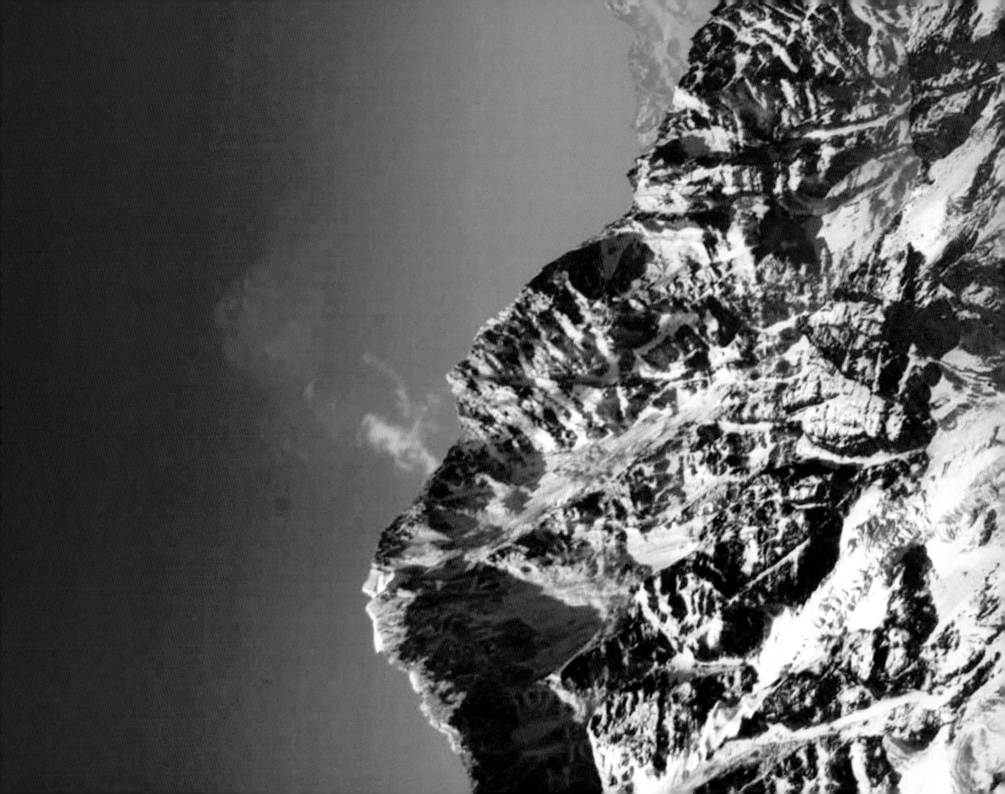

The members of the Weihenmayer's expedition relax and play cards during a break from the climb; even during their moment of fun they continue to wear their oxygen masks.

Facing page: *A resolute Weihenmayer did not stop with the ascent of Everest. He went on to complete the climbs to all Seven Summits—the highest mountains on each of the seven continents.*

Preceding pages: *The year before he made the successful climb to Everest's summit, Weihenmayer reached the summit of Mount Ama Dablam, considered one of the most beautiful peaks. Seen here, Weihenmayer takes a moment to rest en route his ascent up Ama Dablam.*

veteran Everest climbers and trusted friends of Weihenmayer.

After almost two years of preparation, Weihenmayer arrived in the village of Lukla in March 2001. Located at a height of 8000 feet, the village is about 40 miles (nearly 64 km) away from the Everest Base Camp which is at a height of 17,500 feet (5334 m).

Weihenmayer's team comprised ten teammates and eight "indispensable" Sherpa guides. Weihenmayer has on a number of occasions publicly thanked this team, without whom he says he would never have been able to reach the top of Everest.

From Base Camp, the team set out to climb the South Col route, which according to Weihenmayer is "steeped in mountaineering lore and [was] the same way taken by Everest pioneers Sir Edmund Hillary and Tenzing Norgay".

However, once faced with the Khumbu Icefall, Weihenmayer began to question the ideals and optimism that had led him this far. Describing the stretch he says: "A living beast, the icefall slides slowly down the Khumbu Valley, creating an ever-changing landscape as huge chunks of ice, the size of school buses, calve off and shatter below."

After working his way through the Icefall, a battered, bruised and broken Weihenmayer literally stumbled into Camp I—having taken six more than the allotted seven hours. Everyone, including Scaturro, began to have serious doubts about the expedition and its very objective. A determined Weihenmayer, however, was back on his feet the next day and made his way back down through the Icefall. He finally cut his time down from the initial 13 to just 5 hours.

On 20 May, after two months of acclimatisation, four camps, and several traverses in between, later the expedition was yet to make

Weihenmayer with his entire team after summitting Mount Everest. Weihenmayer has time and again expressed the deepest gratitude for all expedition members who made the feat possible.

You Don't Need Sight, What You Need is Vision

Speaking at a Summit County Gathering held to commemorate the 10-year anniversary of his climb, Weihenmayer said, "We all have a lot of goals out here, ambitious goals that keep us busy. But in my life there's been something more important than a goal, what I call vision.... It is more of an internal vision, a vision of how we see ourselves living our lives and serving other people and impacting the world, what kind of legacy we want to leave behind us." This philosophy is what seems to drive Weihenmayer.

Although he is best known for his ascent of Mount Everest, Weihenmayer is a world class athlete who has pushed himself constantly to test his own and other people's perceptions of what people without sight can achieve. Over the years, Weihenmayer has skied down some of the most difficult slopes, paraglided, skydived, completed tandem bike rides and run marathons. He has also accomplished the following feats:

1. By January 2001, before attempting to climb Mount Everest he had scaled Kilimanjaro (19,340 feet/5895 m), Aconcagua (22,834 feet/6962 m), McKinley (20,320 feet/6194 m), and Antarctica's Vinson Massif (16,066 feet/4892 m).

2. In 1999, Weihenmayer joined Mark Wellman—the first paraplegic to climb the 3000-foot (914 m) face of El Capitan—and Hugh Herr—a double-leg-amputee and scientist at Harvard's prestigious prosthetics Laboratory—to climb an 800-foot

By 20 May 2001, Weihenmayer's team was yet to make a bid for the summit. With just 10 days left before the climbing permit expired, his Everest dreams were in jeopardy. But the weather soon cleared and he made it to the summit.

(244 m) rock tower in Moab, Utah.

3. He became the first blind person to complete the Leadville 100 mountain bike race.

4. In September 2003, Weihenmayer joined 320 athletes from 17 countries to compete in the Primal Quest, the richest and toughest multi-sport adventure race in the world. He and his team became one of 42 teams to cross the finish line out of the 80 teams that competed.

Weihenmayer is seen here at Chortan camp with his father Ed Weihenmayer who was instrumental in encouraging him to not let his disability prevent him from living a life of adventure. Also seen is his brother Eddy.
Facing page: *Using his custom-made poles, Weihenmayer's first trip through the Icefall took him thirteen hours; soon he had it down to five hours.*

> By all accounts, Erik is gifted with strong lungs, a refined sense of balance, a disproportionately powerful upper body, rubbery legs and flexible ankles. His conditioning is exemplary and his heart rate low. He is stockier than most mountaineers, who tend toward lanky, long muscles. But he possesses an abundance of the one indispensable characteristic of a great mountaineer: mental toughness, the ability to withstand tremendous amounts of cold, discomfort, physical pain, boredom, bad food, insomnia and tedious conversation when you're snowed into a pup tent for a week on a 3-ft. wide ice shelf at 20,000 ft. ❯❯
>
> **—Karl Taro Greenfeld, "Blind To Failure",** *Time Magazine,* **18 June 2001**

You could do everything right, make few blatant mistakes, and still fall short.

"I worked hard not to buy into the idea that standing on top meant tremendous success while falling a few feet short meant utter failure. This savage unpredictability was the very element I loved and hated about mountains, and made this pursuit an adventure, not just a sport. But even

a bid for the summit. A frustrating wait, because the climbing permit was going to expire at the end of May leaving them with just 10 days in which to realise their ambitions.

Writing in *Touch the Top of the World: A Blind Man's Journey to Climb Farther than the Eye Can See—My Story,* Weihenmayer says of the wait: "For two months, we had been shuttling loads up and down the mountain, while pushing through tremendous doubt and fear. So by mid-May, as time dwindled away, I found myself at Base Camp, awestruck and disappointed as I thought about all we had been through to get to this point. Mike O and I sat in our tent, engaged in long conversations about what constitutes success.

though I could rationalise falling short, it was no less painful."

The weather gods finally turned benevolent and the skies cleared up on 24 May. Using his custom-made climbing poles and listening out for the tinkling bells and instructions from his climbing partners, Weihenmayer and his team set out from Camp IV, making the final push for the summit in the middle of the night. Refusing to be

treated any differently from the other climbers, Weihenmayer finally reached the top of the summit along with all other 18 climbers, setting a record for the maximum number of climbers to summit together—a fitting case for a team that had worked simultaneously as a tight-knit family and a well-oiled machine.

For Weihenmayer, the question of, after Everest what? simply does not arise. He believes that "too many people sit around realising their limitations when, maybe they should spend more time realising their potential." The adventure is far from over. Most recently, Weihenmayer has taken up whitewater kayaking and is focussed on becoming the first blind person to kayak the Grand Canyon.

CHAPTER 10

2005

Min Bahadur Sherchan
Oldest on the Peak

Name: Min Bahadur Sherchan

Age at Time of Ascent: 76 years 340 days

Country of Origin: Nepal

Everest Feat: The oldest person to summit
Mount Everest

No Discrimination
GUINNESS WORLD RECORDS
CERTIFICAT
The record for the most ki
given in one minute is 116
was achieved by Rohit Timil
(Nepal) in Kathmandu, Nepal
on 1 December 2009.
GUINNESS WORLD RECORDS LTD
AIDS, Keep the

" *That's the top of Everest... When I looked down there were only white, shiny clouds and small snow-covered mountains. There was nothing at that height except sun and sky. At that moment, I felt like I was on the top of the world.* **"**

—**Min Bahadur Sherchan**, describing a photograph of himself and his fellow climbers

In May 2005, Min Bahadur Sherchan (extreme left) became the oldest person to summit Everest. Here he is seen with other Nepalese world record holders, Pemba Dorje Sherpa who holds the record for the fastest ascent of Mount Everest (8 hours and 10 minutes), and Khagendra Thapa Magar, the world's shortest teenager.

Due to lack of proper documentary evidence initially, it was only over a year later that the Guinness Book of World Records officially recognised Sherchan's feat. He is seen here with Nepalese Prime Minister Madhav Kumar receiving his certificate.

Facing page: *The mountains, long considered to be the dwelling place of the gods by the local populations of Nepal and Tibet, were out of bounds to human explorations for years. Seen here, ancient stones carved with Buddhist mantras near Dingboche in Nepal.*

Following page: *Ascent from the Eastern side via the Kangshung face is more difficult than climbing from the North Col or the South Col routes. The first successful ascent of it took place only in 1983, 30 years after Everest was first conquered. Seen here, a camp at the height of 24,606 feet (7500 m) on the Kangshung face.*

The year was 1960. Only seven years had passed since Edmund Hillary and Tenzing Norgay had made history by becoming the first climbers to successfully complete an ascent to the summit of Mount Everest. The inspiring feat was still fresh in everyone's memory. And climbing Everest became a dream for the 30-year-old Min Bahadur Sherchan. By then, he was almost too old, at least by Nepalese standards, to even think of achieving great record-breaking mountaineering feats. Nevertheless, age and the fact that he was yet to successfully scale any significant peaks did not deter him from setting for himself a goal of achieving a mountaineering record.

It took him almost 48 years to set that much coveted record. On 25 May 2008, at the age of 76 years and 340 days, Sherchan became the oldest person to stand atop the world's highest mountain. "I was determined to either climb the peak or die trying," he says.

He had many decades ago set his sights on another peak. By 1960, there had been a total of seven unsuccessful attempts on the 26,795 feet (8167 m) high Dhaulagiri, the seventh highest peak in the world, located in central Nepal. There was to be an eighth expedition to Dhaulagiri and Sherchan was appointed to accompany the Swiss expedition as a government liaison officer. That's when his dream

began. He is said to have secretly wished that the expedition would fail so that he could one day become the first person to scale one of the world's highest peaks. However, the expedition was a success with 10 climbers—four foreigners and six Sherpas—reaching the summit. Sherchan was not one of them; for the next 40 years he would not revisit his goal of setting a mountaineering record.

A former soldier in the British Army's Gurkha regiment, Sherchan had always been fit and active but was neither a compulsive nor consummate mountaineer, like several of the other Everest record holders. Born on 20 June 1931 in Nepal's Myagdi district, Sherchan was hardly known in the climbing community at all, which to an extent explains a general sense of surprise at his extraordinary feat.

As a matter of fact, it was a while before Sherchan was officially recognised as the oldest person to successfully summit Mount Everest (see *The Age Controversy: Record Set but Not Recognised*, page 197).

That accolade was mistakenly awarded to renowned Japanese climber and extreme skier Yuichiro Miura, who at the age of 75 years scaled the summit the very next day after Sherchan.

Miura, who is best known as the first man to ski down the slopes of Mount Everest, had previously set the record for the oldest person atop Mount Everest when he climbed the mountain in 2003 as a sprightly 70 year

The Age Controversy: Record Set but Not Recognised

Before Sherchan's feat, all records for the oldest people to climb Everest were held by Japanese nationals. It was Sherchan's dream that this record should belong to a Nepalese national.

Nepal's Min Bahadur Sherchan climbed the world's highest mountain in May 2008 at the age of 76 years and 340 days and believed that in doing so he had become the oldest person in the world to do so. But when the Guinness Book of World Records came out in 2009, it credited another climber with the feat. The name listed was that of Yuichiro Miura, who had scaled the peak the day after Sherchan at the age of 75 years 227 days.

Termed as an oversight and a misunderstanding, the reason behind the exclusion of Sherchan's name from official records was that he had failed to provide the necessary documentary evidence of his achievement. Sherchan had not realised that he had to put together the claim himself, he had assumed that the Nepalese authorities would do it for him. A tenacious Sherchan fought back and sent the authorities at the Guinness Book of World Records all the necessary documentation, including photos, eyewitness verifications and media reports to confirm the veracity of his ascent and its claim. In August 2009, his claim was accepted by the authorities and Sherchan received the hallowed certificate at a formal ceremony organised by the Nepalese government.

The World at Her Feet

Name: Tamae Watanabe

Country of Origin: Japan

Age at Time of Ascent: 63 (2002), 73 (2012)

Everest Feat: Oldest woman to summit Everest

She's done it not once, but twice. In 2002, the 63-year-old Tamae Watanabe became the oldest woman to summit Mount Everest. Ten years later, when she should have been enjoying a typically gentle life of a retired citizen, Watanabe decided it was time to surpass her own achievement.

In 2012 she was back. A decade older, and still, it would seem, as fit and determined as before, she decided to scale the world's highest mountain from the northern slope on the Tibetan-Chinese side. Her previous feat had been achieved from the southern slope in Nepal. Climbing through the night with four other team members, on the morning of 19 May 2012 the 73 years and 180 days old Watanabe once again stood on top of the world, beating her own previous record by a remarkable 10 years. This, despite having broken her back in 2005—an accident from which many thought that she would never recover.

During the 1970s, Watanabe began a personal quest of sorts which included climbing some of the world's highest mountains. Till now, she has scaled 5 of the 14 mountains higher than 26,246 feet (8000 m), including McKinley in North America and Dhaulagiri in Nepal.

Japanese mountaineer Tamae Watanabe bettered her own 10-year-old record of being the oldest woman to reach the top of the world's highest mountain, when she climbed Everest on 19 May 2012 at the age of 73.

Sherchan was chosen as the leader of the Senior Citizens Mount Everest Expedition (SECEE) Nepal 2008. The SECEE Nepal 2008—a not-for-profit social organisation registered and recognised by the government of Nepal—was set up with the explicit purpose of being an "Everest expedition in the service of senior citizens of Nepal, their respect and pride".

Belonging to the Thakali tribe of Nepal, Sherchan was 72 years old when he started training for what was to be an achievement of a lifetime. His doctors were sceptical of his success and felt that his body at his age could not take the altitude pressure of more than 9800 feet (3000 m). To prove them wrong, he went on to climb a 16,404 foot-high (5000 m) peak within Nepal. Sherchan's dream seems to have been part whim, part nationalism and part social

old. In fact, his record was subsequently broken by yet another Japanese man, Katsusuke Yanagisawa who successfully made it to the top of the world's highest mountain in May 2007 at the age of 71 years.

Interestingly, until Sherchan's record-breaking feat, the only climbers over 70 to summit Everest had been from Japan. This fact seemed to provide the 70-year-old Sherchan with just enough motivation to attempt the feat himself. He felt that since it was his fellow countrymen who (at that point in time) held the records for the youngest, fastest and most climbs on Everest, the record for the oldest person on Everest too should belong to a Nepalese. When he finally made it to the top of the world's highest mountain, Sherchan says he felt, "as if I was even higher than Mount Everest".

activism, rather than being borne of a burning sense of personal ambition. After the climb, he stated, "My main objective for climbing Everest was for world peace."

A hero in his own country, there is very little that is known about this diminutive man outside Nepal. News reports are few and far between, the interviews primarily in Nepalese and he's neither a professional motivational speaker nor has he penned his autobiography. But that does not faze Sherchan, who plans to climb Mount Everest yet again, this time at the age of 84. That is the age at which, according to the lore of the Thakali community, an elder becomes an incarnation of God. What better way to celebrate this landmark birthday than by walking with the gods atop the world's highest mountain.

A stunning evening view of Mount Everest and one of her sister peaks, Nuptse (the other being Lhotse) from Kala Patthar mountain in Nepal.

Previous page: *Sherchan broke the record set by 71-year-old teacher and mountaineer from Japan, Katsusuke Yanagisawa to become the oldest person to summit Everest. Seen here is Yanagisawa, who scaled the mountain in May 2007.*

*American teenager Jordan Romero became the
youngest person to reach the summit of Mount
Everest on 21 May 2010. He was 13 years old.*

Can't Drive, Can't Vote, But Can Climb

Name: Jordan Romero

Country of Origin: United States of America

Age at Time of Ascent: 13 years

Everest Feat: Youngest person to summit Everest

Pre-occupied with video games, most 13-year-old American boys are happy to kick a ball around their backyard in the name of physical exercise. But not Jordan Romero. When he was 13, Romero was busy creating mountaineering history by becoming the youngest person in the world to summit the world's tallest mountain.

Updating his blog from Everest Base Camp, Romero wrote: "Today I leave Base Camp… and every step I take is finally toward the biggest goal of my life, to stand on top of the world… I feel in some way I have succeeded in just getting this far, but on the other hand I am drawn to do something great. Know that it comes from my heart. I hope to make you all proud."

When, after a seven-day climb, Romero finally reached the peak on 22 May 2010, he called his mother on the satellite phone to say: "Mom, I'm calling you from the top of the world."

Having previously scaled Africa's Mount Kilimanjaro when he was just 10 year old, Romero set himself the target of scaling the highest peak in each of the seven continents. With the Everest success in his pocket, he had only Vinson Massif in Antarctica left to scale before laying claim to being the youngest in the world to complete the ascent of Seven Summits.

In December 2011, 15-year-old Romero reached the top of the 16,066 feet (4,897 m) high Vinson Massif in Antarctica to fulfill his ambition of climbing the highest mountains on each of the seven continents. Seen here training in Big Bear Lake, California in April 2010.

Undoubtedly a remarkable feat in itself, Romero's climb did spark a serious debate about child climbers and the parental responsibility that comes with it. Since Nepal does not allow anyone under the age of 16 to climb Mount Everest, Romero's team decided to scale the mountain from the Chinese side, where there are no age restrictions.

Elizabeth Hawley in 2008 scanning her biography, I'll Call You in Kathmandu. *She is surrounded by her mountaineering files, extensive library and a tabletop of international awards in the Dilli Bazaar apartment where she has lived since first settling in Nepal in 1960.*

Elizabeth Hawley

A Life Chronicling Himalayan Expeditions

By Lisa Choegyal

Miss Elizabeth Hawley is the undisputed, unofficial authority on Himalayan mountaineering in Nepal, a "one-woman mountaineering institution" who has systematically collected and compiled a detailed database of expeditions since she came to live in Kathmandu in 1960. She has never climbed a mountain, but is respected by mountaineers worldwide. Lisa Choegyal, who has known her for 35 years, reflects on the achievements of this famously formidable 89 year old.

An American journalist living in Nepal since 1960, Elizabeth Hawley is recognised worldwide as the "high priestess of posterity" when it comes to expedition records. As adventurer Eric Hansen writes in *Outside* magazine: "It doesn't matter if you're Reinhold Messner, Chris Bonington, David Breashears or Ed Viesturs: your summit never happened unless Elizabeth Hawley says it did."

Her records of mountaineering information are trusted by newswires, scholars, alpine clubs and climbing publications worldwide. The American Alpine Club publishes her database, the BBC interviews her, and *Outside* magazine recently featured her achievements. To celebrate the diamond jubilee of the first ascent of Everest in 1953, Elizabeth will be featured in a new U.S. documentary, and her 2005 biography *I'll Call You in Kathmandu* is being updated by its author, Bernadette McDonald. There is interest in printing her monthly political summaries that she prepared for Jim Edwards, adventure travel pioneer, as part of her job as director of Tiger Tops and Mountain Travel Nepal during the 1980s and 1990s.

A living treasure

Over the years, the work of Elizabeth has been formally recognised by many organisations including the American Alpine Club, New Zealand Alpine Club and Nepal Mountaineering Association. She has received the King Albert I Memorial Foundation medal, and she was the first recipient of the Sagarmatha National Award from the Government of Nepal. The American Ambassador, Peter Bodde, considers her one of Nepal's "living treasures". "Her contribution to the depth of knowledge and understanding between Nepal and the U.S. is immense," he told me.

In 2004 she received the Queen's Service Medal for Public Services for her work as New Zealand honorary consul and executive officer of Sir Edmund Hillary's Himalayan Trust. With typical modesty she told me: "I was totally astonished... It is a very pleasant feeling".

A diminutive figure of slight build with a keen look, Elizabeth seems bemused at the universal attention she receives. In an interview I did with her for the Royal Geographical Society some years back, I described her "passion" for collecting mountaineering facts. "Lisa, please remove that word from the article," she barked. "I am simply an historian—I am not passionate about ANYTHING!"

The second summit

Elizabeth Hawley's files clutter her modest first floor flat in central Kathmandu. They are her life's work, containing detailed information about more than 80,000 ascents of about 340 Nepalese peaks, including those that border China and India. Over the course of some 15,000 expedition interviews, she has not only recorded history but her research work has also sparked and resolved controversies. She has seen the Nepal climbing scene transformed from an exclusive cult to a mainstream obsession. Though some mountaineers are intimidated by her interrogations—sometimes jokingly referred to as an expedition's "second summit",—all serious alpinists greatly admire her.

"If I need information about climbing 8000-metre peaks, I go to her," says Italian climbing legend Reinhold Messner. "She has everything."

"She's the queen," says Beth Heller, director of the American Alpine Club Library. "There is nothing else like her records."

Nepali mountain guide, Great Himalaya Trailblazer and environmental activist Dawa Steven Sherpa says that Miss Hawley plays a vital role in authenticating climbs. "Although it's the Tourism Ministry that should be doing this, they're not doing it as strictly as Miss Hawley," he says. "One of her biggest contributions is keeping the mountaineers honest."

Elizabeth hardly fits the profile of a "chronicler of climbing". Even in her youth she scarcely hiked. "I don't like trekking at all," she says. "I like to sleep in a comfortable bed, eat hot food in a chair at a table and drive around in the Beetle"—her iconic 1960s blue Volkswagen bug. Essentially an historian who studied at the University of Michigan, she has been researching and documenting Himalayan climbs since 1963 and has the reputation of being an authoritative, sharp-tongued judge who does not suffer fools.

"I don't mean to frighten people, but maybe I've acquired this aura of being the arbitrator," she says. "It might scare them into telling me the truth and that might be useful. Climbers like to be in the database, they like to have their name in print amongst other mountaineers."

"I came to Nepal. I never planned to stay. I just never left."

Elizabeth first arrived in Nepal via India for a couple of weeks in February 1959, on a two-year round the world trip that took her to Eastern Europe, the Middle East and South Asia. Bored with her job as researcher-reporter with *Fortune* magazine in New York, she cashed her savings and travelled as far as they lasted.

"Nepal had been in my mind since reading a 1955 *New York Times* article about the first tourists to the then-kingdom," she remembers. With her media contacts, the *Time–Life Delhi* bureau chief asked her to report on Nepal's politics. It was a most interesting time—as one of only four foreign journalists, she was present when King Mahendra handed over the first parliamentary constitution, which paved the way for democracy in Nepal. Fascinated by Nepal's politics and the idea of an isolated state emerging into the 20th century, she returned in 1960 accredited as a part time correspondent for *Time-Life*, and two years later for *Reuters News Agency*. "I'm still here in the very same house, and have no plans to leave!"

In those days she recalls there were very few cars in the Valley, no streetlights and the roads were mostly unpaved. She rode about town on a bicycle. Telephones were scarce, and all international communication was by telegram—there were lots of funny incidents of reporters competing to file stories. There were very few shops. She had many contacts in government and was very much a "political animal", driven by her interest in what was going on in the country: "I

was privileged to witness many historic events. I knew legendary figures such as Boris Lissanevitch, the charming proprietor of the Royal Hotel, and Peter Aufschnaiter of *Seven Years in Tibet* fame. Col Jimmy Roberts, the climber and founder of the trekking industry, was a special friend and really helped me in those early days to understand how mountaineering worked."

Vital resource

Her interest in collecting mountaineering data started almost by accident. "I've never climbed

Highly regarded by mountaineers the world over for her reliable records and exacting standards, Elizabeth Hawley is pictured debating with legendary climber, Reinhold Messner, whom she holds in particularly high regard.

In 2003, the Mount Everest Golden Jubilee Celebrations took place with much fanfare throughout Kathmandu. The event marked the 50th anniversary of Edmund Hillary and Tenzing Norgay's ascent of Everest on 29 May 1953. Seen here are Reinhold Messner, Sir Edmund Hillary and his wife June, and Japanese Junko Tabei, the first woman to climb Everest.

a mountain, or even done much trekking." As part of her Reuter's job she began to report on mountaineering activities and that's how it started. In those pioneering days of first ascents and mountain exploration, there was a lot of media interest in expeditions.

"Since 1963 I have been meeting every expedition to the Nepal Himalaya both before and after their ascents, including those who climb from Tibet. That's a lot of expeditions! Since those early

days, it became a habit and I have just kept going. I keep biographical details of every expedition member, Nepalis as well as foreigners, and list facts such as who went to what altitude when, and any unusual incidents for every expedition. My education as an historian means that collection of data and statistics appeals to me, although I consider myself a reporter rather than a writer."

Even though she has just passed her 89th birthday and last year broke her hip, Elizabeth still manages to meet mountaineers. She has a number of multi-lingual assistants, including German climber Billi Bierling, and Narmita Shrestha who updates the computer. "It is a bit hectic during the climbing seasons, but I like being busy. I have a wonderful driver, Suben, who takes me around the small hotels in Thamel where the mountaineers stay. These days some come to visit me in the flat. Most difficult are the climbers who don't speak much English—we have to make do with sign language and pictures!"

Incredible ascents

She is interested in the human dimension of why people climb mountains, and how mountains affect people—over the years she has had the opportunity to know so many, and watched them grow and change. "I particularly admire Reinhold Messner with his articulate passion and ecstasy for mountains, and the great leadership qualities of Chris Bonington.

"The most incredible ascents are not just the most historic," Elizabeth explains. "The first attempt in 1921, or the first successful one in 1953, or the first woman in 1975. These were bound to happen—it was just a question of when and by whom.

"But the totally unexpected—the first and only truly solo ascent in 1980 (Reinhold Messner) and the first ascent by a blind person in 2001 (Erik Weihenmayer), with special mention of the first resurrection in 1996 (Beck Weathers) though he had not gone all the way to the summit. These were not inevitable, and therefore I found them incredible."

She says the hardest part of her job is recording accidents and mountaineering deaths. "You remember them, you mention them in dispatches, you go on," she says.

Everest Diamond Jubilee

Sir Edmund Hillary has described Elizabeth Hawley as "a most remarkable person" and "a woman of great courage and determination."

He was one of her oldest friends and she is one of his greatest admirers. "I began working with Ed and the Himalayan Trust in the mid-1960s, dispensing the funds he raises to build hospitals, schools, bridges, forest nurseries and scholarships for the people of Solu Khumbu. He and his wife June used to visit Nepal every year and stay in the Himalayan Trust office apartment downstairs in her house.

"I have been through a lot together with Ed. Good times, such as his 80th birthday dinner in Wellington as the guest of the Governor General, and the 50th anniversary celebrations of the first ascent of Everest in Kathmandu which he so greatly enjoyed. And tragic times, such as when I had to fly by helicopter to tell him that his wife and daughter had been killed in a plane crash—it was the worst week of my life." I travelled with Elizabeth to the sad but magnificently inspiring occasion of Sir Ed's State Funeral in Auckland in January 2008.

"Sir Edmund Hillary is the finest person I ever met," she says with pride.

Lisa Choegyal has been in the tourism business for over 35 years. Based in Kathmandu Nepal, she works throughout the Asia Pacific region as a consultant in planning and developing pro-poor responsible tourism. With a background in the private sector as director of the Tiger Mountain group where she first worked with Elizabeth Hawley, Lisa is author of several books on Nepal including Kathmandu Valley Style and Offerings from Nepal and produced the original South Asia editions of the Insight Guide series. She took over from Elizabeth Hawley as New Zealand Honorary Consul to Nepal in 2010.

CHAPTER 11

On Dangerous Ground

Tragedies on Mount Everest

7 June 1922: 7 Sherpas die in what become the first recorded deaths on Everest

8 June 1924: George Leigh Mallory and Andrew Irvine disappear while climbing Everest. Mallory's body is found 75 years later; Irvine's is still missing.

10-11 May 1996: 8 climbers die on Everest as a result of a freak snowstorm and overcrowding on the mountain. Seven other people perish during the year, making it the worst year in Everest history.

May 2006: 11 people die in a single month while attempting to climb Everest. Increasing number of commercial expeditions criticised.

April-May 2012: 10 climbers die and there are at least two dozen helicopter evacuations. Calls for stricter climbing regulations increase.

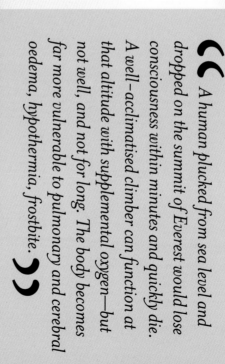

❝ A human plucked from sea level and dropped on the summit of Everest would lose consciousness within minutes and quickly die. A well-acclimatised climber can function at that altitude with supplemental oxygen—but not well, and not for long. The body becomes far more vulnerable to pulmonary and cerebral oedema, hypothermia, frostbite. **❞**

—**Jon Krakauer in** Into Thin Air

Given the treacherous topography and extreme weather conditions, retrieving bodies from Mount Everest is an extremely difficult task, and those above 8000 metres are usually left undisturbed on the mountain itself. Seen here is the body of a mountaineer being retrieved by unseen Sherpas during the Everest clean-up expedition in May 2010, led by seven-time summiteer Namgyal Sherpa.

While a handful have dared to, and succeeded, in reaching the summit without any supplemental oxygen, a significant majority of Everest climbers rely heavily on their oxygen apparatus. Seen here, a mountaineer checks on the oxygen supplies.

Facing page: *George Leigh Mallory's body was found in 1999 at 26,575 feet (8100 m). 75 years after he disappeared with fellow climber Andrew Irvine. Due to the below freezing temperatures and permanent ice at that height, Mallory's body as well as the clothes and other artifacts on him were found to be in a state of remarkable preservation.*

Standing 29,029 feet (8848 m) above sea level—the highest point on earth—is an exciting and admirable ambition. It is also one that is fraught with peril. Crevasses hundreds of feet deep, massive avalanches, dangerously slippery ice, treacherously narrow ridges, ever shifting rivers of ice, and the constant danger of hypothermia and the fear of succumbing to any number of high-altitude related sicknesses are only some of the stumbling blocks that stand between the mountaineer and Mount Everest's summit.

While thousands of men and women have made this perilous journey up and then down the mountain safely, a number of them have not been so fortunate. The mountain does not discriminate between those it claims. To date, close to 300 people, including porters, guides, amateur climbers and professional mountaineers from across nations have perished on the treacherous and unforgiving slopes of Mount Everest. Some have fallen to their deaths, some have died of exposure to the elements, while a small handful have simply disappeared, leaving posterity to piece together the reasons for their death.

The first recorded deaths in the history of Everest climbing were those of the seven Sherpas who lost their lives in a massive avalanche on 7 June 1922. The Sherpas were part of the Second British Everest Expedition, which was attempting to scale Everest from the North side.

The first and still the most famous "disappearance" is that of British climbers George Mallory and Andrew "Sandy" Irvine. The pair was last spotted just after midday on 8 June 1924 by fellow climber Noel Odell, somewhere in the vicinity of the First Step at

28,097 feet (8564 m), just under 1000 feet (around 284 m) from the summit. In their wake, they left the most enduring of Everest mysteries: Were they the first people to summit Mount Everest? While Mallory's body was found in 1999, Irvine's remains are still buried somewhere on the slopes of the world's highest mountain.

The worst recorded year in Everest climbing came 72 years later. In May 1996, the mountain was particularly overcrowded with guide-led climbing expeditions, threatening the safety of all those attempting to summit the mountain. Members from two guided expeditions—Rob Hall and his Adventure Consultants and the Scott Fischer-led Mountain Madness—and a Taiwanese government-sponsored expedition

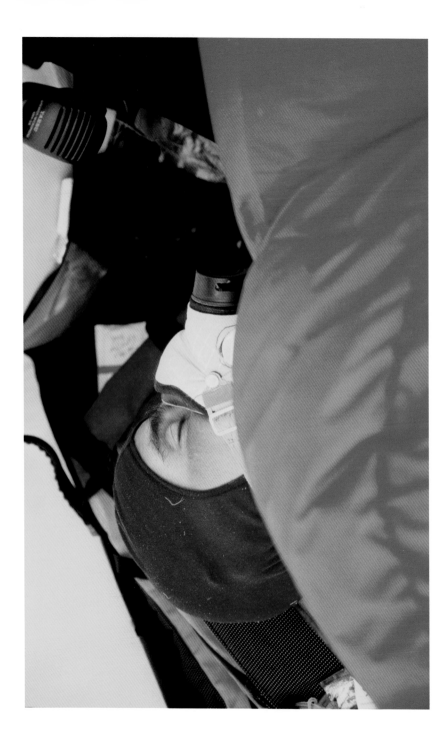

all began a summit attempt from Camp IV at the height of 25,918 feet (7,900 m) just after midnight on 10 May. There were problems from the very beginning of this leg of the climb. Miscommunication and lack of coordination amongst the various groups led to Sherpa guides failing to set the fixed line ropes both across the Balcony as well as the Hillary Step, slowing down the climbers. In addition, 33 climbers queuing up to reach the summit meant a severe bottleneck at the Hillary Step, which is at a height of 28,740 feet (8,760 m). This in turn meant that all climbers, irrespective of aptitude and experience, had to spend more time than is advisable in the Death Zone with fast depleting oxygen reserves. Despite this, climbers and guides pushed their way to

the summit, oblivious to the drastically changing weather conditions. In a blatant disregard of the predetermined turnaround times—a necessary precaution for the safety of all climbers—some of the climbers and their guides arrived on the summit much later than scheduled.

Meanwhile, the hitherto benign weather seemed to change almost abruptly, with strong winds turning ferocious and temperatures and oxygen levels plummeting to dangerous levels almost immediately. The worsening weather began causing difficulties for the descending team members. By the night of 11 May, the blizzard on the Southwest Face of Everest was in full blow, reducing visibility to near zero and erasing all signs that marked the trail back to safety.

In all, five climbers died on the South side of the mountain while three perished on the North Ridge. Those who died on the South side were Andrew Harris from New Zealand, Doug Hansen from the United States, Yasuko Namba from Japan and expedition leaders New Zealander Rob Hall and American Scott Fischer. Those who lost their lives on the north side were members of an Indo-Tibetan expedition and include: Subedar Tsewang Samanla, Lance Naik Dorje Morup and Head Constable Tsewang Paljor. Seven other people died in their summit bids at other times of the year, making it the deadliest single year in Mount Everest's history.

In his detailed account of the incident, *Into Thin Air*, journalist Jon Krakauer has suggested that the use of bottled oxygen and commercial guides were two reasons that made a difficult situation catastrophic. Guides felt obliged to push fee-paying clients beyond their limits in order to deliver what they had been promised. In the same book, he is also critical of the regulations that allow climbers with limited or almost no previous mountaineering experience to undertake this perilous climb, endangering not just themselves but also all others on the mountain.

With none of the issues that exacerbated the 1996 disaster being resolved, another disaster struck the slopes of Mount Everest in May 2006. That year a total of 11 people perished in one month alone. The most talked about death was

---

U.S. CLIMBER'S DEATH ON EVEREST

JACKSON, WYOMING, March 25.—Mrs. John Breitenbach said today she had received a telegram from the State Department in Washington informing her that her husband had been killed while climbing Mount Everest. Efforts had been made to recover the body, but had to be abandoned because of the "large mass of ice covering it", the telegram said.

KATMANDU, March 25.—The American Everest team, which left here on February 20, has set up base camp at 17,800ft. on the Khumbu glacier, according to a radio message received here today.—Reuter.

Storm halts attempt on Everest

From Ronald Faux
Shyangboche, April 28

A severe storm on Everest has forced a halt in the first attempt to climb the mountain without 29,028ft

---

MT. EVEREST TRAGEDY.

TWO CLIMBERS KILLED.

FATE OF MR. MALLORY AND MR. IRVINE.

("The Times" World Copyright.)

The Mount Everest Committee have received, with profound regret, the following telegram from Lieut.-Colonel E. F. Norton, the leader of the expedition, dispatched from Phari Dzong on June 19, at 4.50 p.m.:—

"Mallory and Irvine killed on last attempt. Rest of party arrived at base camp all well."

The Committee have telegraphed to Colonel Norton, expressing their deep sympathy with the expedition in the loss of their two gallant comrades, which must have been due to the most unfavourable conditions of weather and snow which have from the first arrival at the scene of operations impeded the climbing this year. The last message from Colonel Norton, dated May 26, told how the party had been driven out of their high camp for the second time by heavy snow. It seems probable that they had been able to return to the assault early in this month, and that the lamentable accident which has cost the lives of two of the best climbers occurred about June 6.

The tragic death of these two men—George Leigh Mallory, who alone of all

---

News reports from the Times on the snowstorm that temporarily halted Reinhold Messner and Peter Habeler's attempt to scale Everest without oxygen (Saturday, 29 April 1978); informing the world of George Mallory and Andrew Irvine's disappearance on the slopes of Mount Everest (Saturday, 21 June 1924) and telling of the death of American climber John Breitenbach, member of the 1963 National Geographic Society sponsored American Mount Everest Expedition (Tuesday, 26 March 1963).

Facing page: *The conditions on Everest are so extreme that even experienced climbers such as Vern Tejas have to sleep with an oxygen mask in their tent on the South Col of Mount Everest, to reduce the risk of high altitude sickness setting in.*

A severe snowstorm hits Camp III at an altitude of 22,000 feet (6705 m) on the West Ridge of Mount Everest, reducing visibility to near zero. A snowstorm is only one of the many potentially fatal natural disasters that stare in the face of each climber attempting to scale Everest.

Facing page: *Woven into the tragedy of loss of human lives is also a narrative of acts of bravery and heroism by the most ordinary of men. Seen here, a porter has cut his doko (straw basket) to accommodate an injured expedition member at Thokla Pass. The injured member was carried down from Base Camp to Namche Bazaar, a two-day hard walk down, from where he was airlifted by helicopter to Kathmandu.*

that of Briton David Sharp (see *A Man and his Incredible Feat*, pages 164–167) who lay dying from exposure just 984 feet (300 m) short of the summit, with 40 climbers walking past him.

After a six-year period, yet another mishap struck on the mountain. Described by those who were there as "overcrowded" and "gridlocked", Mount Everest claimed four lives in just two days in May 2012. An estimated 150 climbers reached the summit on those days, most of them on Saturday. The victims included Ebehard Schaaf, a German medical doctor; Sriya Shah, a Nepali-born Canadian woman; Song Wondin from South Korea; and Wen Ryi Ha of China. There were six other fatalities in the season as well as several serious injuries that resulted in roughly two dozen

helicopter evacuations. In all, 10 people perished on Everest in April and May of 2012, making it the third deadliest year in record.

What is of growing concern is that the deaths are no longer due to freak weather conditions or incorrect meteorological reports; they are increasingly due to ill-preparedness and inexperience of amateur climbers who are more akin to tourists than to serious high altitude mountaineers. There are also serious reservations about the increasing number of people on the slopes of Everest every season. This overcrowding leads to long delays and commercialisation leads to disregard for safety in favour of promised summit glory and a general sense of false bravado amongst many would-be climbers.

Mount Everest: A Timeline
Climbing Triumphs and Tragedies

1841

Sir George Everest, Surveyor General of India from 1830 to 1843 records the exact location of Mount Everest. In 1856 surveyor **Andrew Waugh** completes the first height measurement of the mountain, declaring Everest to be 29,002 feet (8840 m) high. In 1865, the mountain formerly known as Peak XV is re-named Mount Everest to honour Sir George Everest.

1921

The first British Everest Reconnaissance Expedition to the mountain is led by **Lt Colonel Charles Howard-Bury.** After ten weeks of exploring the northern and eastern reaches of the mountain, on 24 September 1921, **Guy Bullock** and **George Mallory** become the first climbers to reach the North Col of Everest at an altitude of around 23,000 feet (7000 m).

1922

The Second British Everest Expedition to the mountain is led by **Brigadier General C.G. Bruce. George Mallory** is accompanied by climbers George Finch, Geoffrey Bruce, Henry Morshead, Edward Norton, Howard Somervell, and John Noel as expedition filmmaker. Over a two week period three assaults are made towards the summit, with George Finch and Geoffrey Bruce climbing up the North Ridge and Face to 27,300 feet (8320 m) feet using oxygen. Seven Sherpa climbers lose their lives in an avalanche below the North Col in what became the first reported deaths on Everest.

1924

On the morning of 8 June, British climbers **George Leigh Mallory** and **Sandy Irvine** set out from their camp at 26,700 feet (8,138 m) on the Northeast Ridge. They are last seen hours later, "moving expeditiously" toward the summit by fellow climber Noel Odell. Debates about whether they were the first to summit Everest continue to this day.

1950

The Chinese invade Tibet, and the northern approach to the mountain, used by all previous expeditions, is shut off to Westerners.

1952

A Swiss expedition, with climbers **Raymond Lambert** and **Sherpa Tenzing Norgay** follow the South Col, or South-East Ridge route, and get to within 800 feet (150 m) of the summit before weather conditions force them to turn back.

1953

On 29 May, New Zealander **Edmund Hillary** and **Sherpa Tenzing Norgay** from Nepal make history by becoming the first men to stand on the summit of Mount Everest.

1956

The Swiss expedition of 1956 puts the next four climbers on the summit. Their feat includes the first successful ascent of Lhotse.

1960

A Chinese expedition team claims a first successful ascent of the mountain's North Ridge, but the claim remains unsubstantiated as there is no evidence that the team went beyond the Second Step.

1963

Jim Whittaker, accompanied by **Nawang Gombu Sherpa**, becomes the first American to summit the mountain. The same year Americans Tom Horbein and Willi Unsoeld become the first to ascend the West Ridge.

1965

A 21-man Indian expedition, led by **Lieutenant Commander M.S. Kohli** succeeds in putting nine men on the summit. **Nawang Gombu Sherpa** becomes the first person to reach the summit twice, first with an American expedition in 1963 and second with an Indian expedition in 1965.

1970

Japanese **Yuichiro Miura** becomes the first man to ski down the slopes of Everest. He does so from the South Col.

1975

Japanese climber **Junko Tabei** becomes the first woman to reach the summit. Her team uses the South Col route. Eleven days later Tibetan woman, Phantog, becomes the first woman to reach the summit from the Tibetan side.

1978

Reinhold Messner (Italy) and Peter Habeler (Austria) become the first climbers to summit the mountain without using supplementary oxygen.

1980

Reinhold Messner returns to Mount Everest to successfully make the first solo ascent, again without supplementary oxygen. He climbs during the August monsoon season for three days alone from his base camp at 6500 metres. Earlier in the year Andrzej Zawada's team from Poland, including Leszek Cichy and Krzysztof Wielicki, make the first successful winter ascent.

1982

A series of deaths take place on Mount Everest. British mountaineers **Peter Boardman** and **Joe Tasker** disappear between the previously unclimbed First and Second Pinnacles on the Northeast Ridge. A Canadian expedition loses their cameraman in an icefall and three Sherpas to an avalanche. American **Marty Hoey** falls to her death from the North Side and veteran Japanese climbers Yasuo Kato and Toshiaki Kobayashi die near the summit in bad weather.

1983

Lou Reichardt and his American teammates claim the first ascent of the daunting Kangshung (East) Face.

1984

Bulgarian **Hristo Prodanov** makes the first ever ascent of the West Ridge Direct without oxygen and climbing solo. He climbs the West Ridge proper and doesn't go through the Hornbein couloirs, opening up a new route on the West Ridge.

1986

Erhard Loretan and **Jean Troillet** introduce a climbing style called "night naked" when they climb the North Face in a single push without oxygen, ropes, or tents in 42 hours, then a glissade down in under 5 hours. They climbed mostly at night and carried no backpacks above 8000 metres.

1988

Jean-Marc Boivin climbs the Southeast Ridge and straps on a portable paraglider and soars down to Camp II in 11 minutes.

1996

It becomes the worst year in the history of Everest climbing when a deadly storm leaves several climbers stranded. 15 people die, including the most successful guide of his time, Rob Hall. Journalist Jon Krakauer later writes a first hand account *Into Thin Air* about the experience. In the same year **Hans Kammerlander** climbs the mountain from the north side in the record ascent time of just under 17 hours from Base Camp to the summit. He climbs alone without supplementary oxygen and skies down from 7,800 metres.

1998

Tom Whittaker, whose right foot had been amputated, becomes the first disabled person to successfully reach the summit.

1999

Climber **Conrad Anker**, a member of an American research expedition, discovers the body of George Mallory at 26,700 feet (8,138 m) on the North Face. This however does nothing to end the Hillary vs Mallory debate conclusively. **Babu Chiri Sherpa** spends 21 hours and 30 minutes on the summit of Everest setting a new world record. In the same year scientists re-measure the mountain and find that it is actually 29,035 feet tall—7 feet higher than previously recorded.

2000

Babu Chiri Sherpa climbs from Base Camp to the summit in under 17 hours, a south-side speed-ascent record that still stands. Slovenian **Davo Karnicar** becomes the first man to accomplish an uninterrupted ski descent from the summit to the Base Camp; he does this in five hours.

2001

Stefan Gatt becomes the first person to snowboard from the summit of Everest. But he walks part of the way. The very next day Marco Siffredi on his snowboard completes the first-ever uninterrupted descent of Everest on a snowboard from the summit. American **Erik Weihenmayer** becomes the first blind person to reach the summit.

2003

Yuichiro Miura returns to Mount Everest after three decades and at the age of 70 years and 222 days, becomes the oldest person ever to summit Everest. His record is broken few years later.

2004

Pemba Dorje Sherpa makes the world's fastest ascent by scaling the mountain in 8 hours 10 minutes. The previous year he had done the climb in 12 hours 45 minutes only to have his record broken three days later by Sherpa Lakpa Gelu who made the climb in 10 hours 56 minutes.

2005

New Zealander **Mark Inglis** becomes the first person to reach the summit with two artificial legs.

2007

Another Japanese climber, **Katsusuke Yanagisawa** beats Miura's record to become the oldest person to reach the summit. He is 71 years and 61 days old.

2008

Yuichiro Miura attempts to reclaim his title of the oldest person to reach the summit at age 75 years and 227 but is beaten to it by Nepalese climber **Min Bahadur Sherchan** who scaled the mountain aged 76 years and 330 days a day before Miura.

2010

Thirteen-year-old American boy **Jordan Romero** becomes the youngest person ever to climb Everest. He later goes on to complete the "Seven Summits" by the time he is 15.

2011

Apa Sherpa summits Everest for a record 21st time.

2012

Tamae Watanabe from Japan breaks her own record as the oldest woman summiteer when she reaches the top of Everest at age 73 years and 180 days.

Picture Credits

AP Photo: 110, 113, 115, 117, 120-121, 122, 138, 147, 149, 165

Apa Sherpa: 106

Carla Yustak: 156, 160, 161, 170-171

Colin Monteath Hedgehog House: 214

Corbis: 10, 76, 80, 94-95 (centre), 95, 104, 130, 132, 146, 150, 162, 188, 190, 191, 192, 193, 194-195, 196, 197, 198, 199, 200, 201, 202, 203, 208, 212, 213

Getty: 2-3, 4-5, 12-13, 14, 24, 67, 69, 81, 89, 100,105, 112, 118, 123, 124, 126-127, 135, 140, 142, 143, 148, 151, 166, 168, 174, 176, 179, 180, 181, 184, 185, 206, 209, 218, 220-223.

India Picture: 210

Lisa Choegyal: 217

Mary Evans Picture Library: 40, 71, 79, 88, 94

Royal Geographical Society: 1, 6-7, 15, 16, 17, 18, 19, 21, 22, 23, 28, 31, 32, 33, 34, 35, 36, 37, 38, 41, 42-43, 44, 45, 46-47, 48, 49, 50-51, 51, 54, 56, 57, 58, 59, 60, 61, 62, 63, 64-65, 66, 68, 70, 72-73, 78, 82-83, 84, 85, 86, 87, 90, 91, 92-93, 98, 101, 103, 144-145, 178

Shutterstock: 20, 25, 102, 119, 134, 141, 177, 182-183

The Times, London: 211

Tom Whittaker: 8, 9, 11, 154, 157, 158